COMFORT AND CARE IN FINAL ILLNESS

JUNE KOLF has experienced aspects of hospice care both professionally and personally. Her extensive experience with numerous hospice patients and their families makes her well qualified to write this much needed book. Mrs Kolf worked for hospice organizations and agencies in California for more than 12 years, serving as a volunteer coordinator. In the past she also has helped care for her parents and other relatives who have entered hospices. Mrs Kolf is married, with three grown-up daughters, and lives in California with her husband, Jack.

KT-446-538

Overcoming Common Problems Series

For a full list of titles please contact
Sheldon Press, Marylebone Road, London NW1 4DU

Overcoming Common Problems Series

Overcoming Common Problems Series

Overcoming Common Problems

Comfort and Care in Final Illness

June Kolf

616.029
Kol

Published in Great Britain in 2000 by
Sheldon Press, SPCK, Marylebone Road, London NW1 4DU

Copyright © 2000 June Cerza Kolf

First published in the United States of America in 1999
by Fisher Books, 5225 W. Massingale Road, Tucson, AZ 85 743–8416, USA.

All rights reserved. No part of this book may be reproduced
or transmitted in any form or by any means, electronic or
mechanical, including photocopying, recording, or by any
information storage and retrieval system, without permission
in writing from the publisher.

Thank you to the Visiting Nurse Association of Los Angeles
Hospice in the Home Program and ProCare Hospice of Lancaster, California
for permission to reprint the 'Symptoms of Impending Death' information
on pages 112–14, and to Hospice of the East San Gabriel Valley
for permission to reprint the poem on page xi.

British Library Cataloguing-in-Publication Data

A catalogue record for this book is available
from the British Library

ISBN 0–85969–833–5

Typeset by Deltatype Limited, Birkenhead, Merseyside
Printed in Great Britain by
Biddles Ltd, Guildford and King's Lynn

Contents

To my mom and dad, Alphonse and Olga Cerza,
who taught me not only how to live
but how to face death without fear,
with grace, dignity and acceptance.

Thank you to: Bill Fisher and Sarah Trotta for believing in my work and for making the process as painless as possible. Your patience and support have come at a perfect time. And a very special thank you to Meg Morris for listening to me when I needed to talk. Your unconditional support has been a great source of comfort. I feel like I have made a special friend, in addition to gaining a new editor.

During the final rewrite of this book, my husband was diagnosed with inoperable bladder cancer. I relocated from my computer to his side as we began our personal battle with a critical illness. May the strength and comfort we have received from God be yours also.

Introduction

When I was born, people were happy and smiling.
I was the only one crying.
When I died, people were sad and crying.
I was the only one happy and smiling.

Anonymous

A doctor walks slowly into his office with his head down; his demeanour suggests defeat. He sits down behind his desk and looks towards the young woman sitting across from him; he avoids making eye contact.

Clearing his throat, he says, 'All the test results are finally in. It looks like you have a very aggressive strain of lung cancer that won't respond to further treatment.'

Debbie's brow furrows as she tries to understand what the doctor is saying.

'What do you mean?' she asks softly.

'Well,' the doctor answers, still avoiding her eyes, 'I'm afraid nothing more can be done.'

Debbie finally asks, 'Does that mean I'm going to die?'

'It's very probable,' the doctor says, and then his eyes, filled with tears, finally meet hers.

After Debbie's doctor tells her nothing more can be done for her medically, what can she do? What are her choices? How many more opinions should she seek? How will she come to terms with such devastating news? What can her family and friends do to help? How can she spend her remaining time so it is as meaningful and productive as possible?

There are no guaranteed answers to these questions; however, there are guidelines that have proved successful for others. Even after medical experts have reached the conclusion that a patient is medically incurable, it does not mean the patient needs to be without hope. A medical opinion is just that – *an opinion*. Miracles happen. Never stop looking for one!

The human body has marvellous recuperative powers, and even without a miracle, life can still have quality. Patients and their loved ones can have a life of quality physically, emotionally and spiritually in whatever time remains. It can be an exceptionally special period of time, a final gift.

Many times, life-threatening illnesses can be treated or put into remission for long periods. In certain cases, experimental programmes may be appropriate. I do not address those situations. This book is for patients who have been given a terminal diagnosis with no suggestion of recovery or remission.

This book is divided into two distinct sections: one is intended for the patient and one is for the people who are caring for the patient (the carers). Some of the information overlaps, but it is offered from different perspectives to allow for the best possible teamwork. Reading the material from both perspectives is not necessary, but it might be helpful. The more familiar the patient and the carer are with the subject, the easier it becomes to deal with all aspects of a terminal diagnosis.

PART 1
The Patient

1

Physical considerations

A terminal diagnosis brings us face to face with mortality. Whether we realize it or not, we are *all* in the process of dying from the day we are born. However, when we are given a terminal diagnosis, we face the reality of our death actively rather than passively because a tentative time limit has been set on life.

Acceptance

Acceptance of a terminal illness is a result of thinking, talking and perhaps praying about the situation. It is important to accept your situation so you can actively participate in the process of dying. A person who denies the truth has no chance of finding acceptance. Proceed slowly. Attempt only what you can handle each day. Talk to a trusted friend; let your tears express what cannot be put into words. This book is intended to help you reach a point of acceptance, and it offers practical advice to make the days ahead easier.

The final days in a person's life can be a time of peace, sharing and joy – or they can be a time of struggle, tears and pain. Death, like any other life experience, is what you make of it for yourself and your loved ones. You may not be able to control the illness, but you *can* control your attitude. You can fill the time with feelings of hope or bitterness. You can form a community of healing, if not for the body, then for the emotions and spirit. You can enjoy your loved ones, or you can be angry with them. You can appreciate the physical care you receive, or you can lash out with harsh demands. The quality of your life, whether in sickness or in health, depends on you.

Many people find either a new or renewed interest in their spiritual life during critical life events. They find prayer or meditation offers solace and peace when they are otherwise inconsolable. Prayers are answered in a variety of ways, just as healing can occur in a variety of ways. Healing may come in the form of a healed body or in healed relationships. Your prayers may be answered with an inner presence of peace that comes with acceptance or a deepened understanding of death. I hope the following information opens avenues and clears the way for an easier journey.

3

Reactions to a terminal diagnosis

There are a number of reactions to a terminal diagnosis. Although every person's response is different, a progression of reactions is common to most people.

Shock

Shock is usually the first feeling to follow a terminal diagnosis. You probably returned from seeing the doctor in a daze as you tried to grasp the devastating information you received. Shock is nature's anaesthetic. It cushions you from intense pain. Shock wears off gradually as your mind adjusts and accepts the news. In the beginning, the best remedy to work through shock to a point of acceptance is to talk about the diagnosis. As you hear the words and express your feelings, the reality gradually settles in.

Denial

Denial follows closely behind shock. Thoughts such as, 'There must be some mistake' and 'This can't be possible' fill your mind. As you talk and think about your illness, little by little you realize you are facing a life-threatening situation.

Fear

In addition to feeling shock and denial when you are told your illness is not curable, you may be struck with agonizing fear – fear of the future, fear of no longer being in control. Dread engulfs you like a heavy, wet blanket, threatening to suffocate you with every breath. Your stomach churns and you keep wishing you would wake up from this terrifying nightmare. But you are already awake and what you are experiencing is not a nightmare.

What you are experiencing is real life, suddenly appearing in stark black and white. You are wide awake, asking repeatedly, 'Why me?' and 'Why now?' Rarely is a person ready to face the fact their life may be coming to an end. There are always reasons why the time is not right. There are always more things you want to live a little longer to see or do. Possibly you have just started a successful career, had a baby or became a grandparent. You are not ready to die. You bargain with God, make promises, do anything to buy some extra time, while your stomach is clutched tight with fear.

One woman told me that following her terminal diagnosis a dark cloak of fear covered her that was suffocating. The process of dying,

4

rather than death itself, frightened her. It was a fear of the unknown. Fears multiply in the dark crevices of the mind. Get them out into the sunshine before they can 'reproduce' and contaminate your life.

Fear of the unknown is a normal response to a terminal diagnosis. The first step to moving through fear is to acknowledge that you are afraid. Then address each area of concern. For example, if you are afraid you will not be given adequate pain control, talk to your doctor and express your concerns. If you are worried about the financial security of your family, consult a professional for advice. Now your main goal is to savour every moment with your family and friends, and to reach a point of serenity. Fear will only stand in the way.

Get medical facts to ease your fears, settle financial matters, and mend broken relationships so you don't leave any loose ends. The better informed you are, the less insecure and fearful you will be.

I once heard a preacher say that death is merely 'relocation'. Although many may agree, it is not much consolation to the person who is being 'relocated' before he is ready. It is normal to be afraid of death. By talking about your fears instead of repressing them, the point of acceptance is easier to reach. With acceptance can come quality time that is spoken of as the 'final gift'.

A final gift

The first time I heard a terminal patient say his illness was his 'last gift from God', I was shocked. I thought, 'Wait a minute! How could a life-threatening illness be a gift?' But with time and more experience, I began to understand. People who die suddenly do not have the opportunity to get their affairs in order. They are unable to say a final farewell, distribute their belongings, mend broken relationships, express love and straighten out legal and financial matters. Sudden death can come before a person's spiritual life is in order. A terminal diagnosis offers an opportunity to finalize matters in all these areas.

What a waste not to make the most of this time! Take this gift and use it to become closer to your loved ones. Change the 'Why me?' to 'How can I use this time to its fullest?' Spend your time deepening your spiritual beliefs and moving toward acceptance.

Dr Elisabeth Kübler-Ross writes in *Living with Death and Dying* that by working together with loved ones, the process of dying can become a special part of life, a time of deep caring that will make the passage natural and peaceful. 'Acceptance is a feeling of victory, a feeling of peace, of serenity, of positive submission to things we cannot change.'

This final journey can be a time of forming lasting memories and receiving gentle care. Think of this time as a unique period of preparation, for along with the anguish of having to face a terminal diagnosis comes the opportunity to prepare for death. Don't waste any of this precious time. Spend it with loved ones, and share special moments with them you never had time for before.

Medical care

Medical professionals give a terminal diagnosis when they have no more options to offer. This section is meant to help you during the phase of illness immediately following such a diagnosis.

Deciding to stop active treatment

Stopping active treatment, even for a terminal patient, is a difficult task for doctors. The focus of doctors' training is to heal and it is uncomfortable for many of them simply to let nature run its course. To succeed at their profession, they must be self-assured. The very confidence that allows them to perform surgery can stand in the way when they have to give up aggressive treatment. They may feel they have failed if they stop treatment and release a patient to hospice care. Therefore it is up to you to make your wishes known if you decide to stop aggressive treatment.

Do not misunderstand. I am grateful that doctors do not give up easily. When I am ill, I want to know they are doing everything humanly possible to make me well. But when they can no longer cure me or improve my condition, I do not want them to experiment on me and prolong my life if it has become merely an existence. I want their honesty and I want to be sent home to die as comfortably and as peacefully as possible.

Even after aggressive treatment of the disease is stopped, it is still necessary to be under a doctor's care for treatment of symptoms and for comfort measures.

Many people do not realize their physical well-being is in their own hands. Even when you seek medical attention, *the final decision about your treatment is your own.* You can always refuse tests, medication or treatment. Usually, this would be foolish. If you want to be healthy again, and a doctor has the knowledge to help you, it makes sense to follow the doctor's instructions carefully. However, if you feel uncomfortable about the doctor's course of action, or you are making little or no progress, it is perfectly permissible and advisable to seek a second or even a third opinion.

Ask questions

Following a terminal diagnosis, many decisions about medical care need to be faced. You cannot simply go to bed and rest until you get well as you were able to with a cold or flu. You need to be actively involved in your medical care. It is essential for you and your carer to know about all the medical decisions being made and the reasoning behind them. Even if you are in the hospital, try to understand your treatment so when you go home, follow-up care will be easier.

For instance, do not just swallow a pill when it is handed to you. Ask for the name of the drug and the reason for taking it. When you are given a prescription, ask the pharmacist for brochures and extra information. You need to be informed so you can participate in your treatment and healing.

By keeping a close watch, if you choose to seek other medical opinions, you will be able to tell the doctor, 'I take 100 mg of Dilantin™ twice a day for seizures,' instead of, 'Oh, I take a tiny white capsule twice a day for something.' It makes a big difference to your overall care! Do not be afraid to ask questions about your treatment plan.

Research and education

Do as much research about the disease as you are physically able to do. When you leave the doctor's surgery or hospital, find books on your particular illness and learn everything you can about it. Ask about the progression of your disease and gather statistics. Call the free helplines for your particular illness and ask for written material. (See page 121 for a list of some of these telephone numbers.) Find out if there are support groups in your area. If the diagnosis is cancer, call the Imperial Cancer Research Fund and ask for printed material. There are websites for each type of cancer, which include a vast amount of information, chat rooms, suggested reading material, nutritional help, organizations to contact and hospices in your area.

Talk with your doctor

Often, a doctor continues treatment for the mental well-being of the patient. Let your doctor know your wishes. Say if you want to discontinue an experimental treatment, and whether you are more interested in the quality or the quantity of life. Be honest about your needs and your feelings. Doctors respect a patient's wishes when they are aware of them. Many times, both patient and doctor play 'pretend' games to make it easier for each other. Don't get into this situation. If you are unable to confide in your doctor or healthcare team, or feel uncomfortable talking to them about personal matters, it may be time to make a change.

The following tips will help you communicate more effectively with your doctor.

Decide how much information you want

Some people deal better with a situation when they know every detail; others prefer to judge their health by the way they feel. Unless your doctor has known you for a long time, she or he will not know your preferences. It is up to you to clarify what your preferences are at the start. For instance, opposite extremes would be, 'I wish to have full knowledge of my condition, no matter how bad it is.' Or, 'Don't give me any bad news. I want only positive information about my health.'

Understand the information you are given

People who are distressed often do not hear what the doctor tells them. If you are confused, ask your doctor to repeat the information. Ask your doctor to clarify the medical jargon until you understand exactly what you have been told. Take notes or have someone else present who can help you sort through the information.

Ask specific questions

- What exactly is my condition?
- How will it be treated?
- What are my options?
- What are the benefits and side-effects of my options?
- What are the risks?
- What can I expect during the course of my illness?

Ask when it is best to telephone if you have further questions

Most doctors have a particular time when they take telephone calls. It is best to be familiar with their schedules.

In summary, make sure you feel confident about the care you are receiving and are comfortable with your healthcare providers. Be sure you understand your condition. It is important to trust your medical team and feel comfortable talking with them about your illness and preferences.

8

How long?

Naturally, you want to know how much time you have left. Statisticians give averages and doctors state odds, but if someone simply pulled a number out of a hat or flipped a coin, it probably would be just as accurate. Remember, medical professionals can give their opinions, but they are only educated guesses.

A new concept of time

The lack of a definite time span is difficult to accept. Most people tend to live according to a schedule they have created. They have clocks and calendars, routines and agendas. They want to know what time something will happen and on what day of the week, so they can mark it on their calendars. They check their watches all day long. Does this describe you?

Then you are told an event will occur, but it has no date or time. It feels foreign to live with an indefinite deadline. First, you are expected to accept the unacceptable news, and then you are expected to make plans for an unknown date. Is it any wonder the concept is so difficult to grasp? All previous plans must be put on hold. Instead of dinner dates, you now have appointments with specialists. You go for medical treatments instead of shopping and you do not dare make holiday plans for next summer. You are forced to live without schedules – only uncertainties. This is one of the most difficult concepts to accept following a terminal diagnosis. Even on good days, you may feel you are waiting for the proverbial second shoe to drop.

Even though my own father, who was in his eighties, lived two years longer than his terminal diagnosis, at the end we wanted to hang on to him two extra weeks so he could celebrate his fifty-third wedding anniversary with Mom. We forgot to be thankful for the additional two years we had with him. Instead, we felt cheated out of those two weeks.

Human beings hold on tightly to their physical lives. We think of death as a thief rather than a natural conclusion to life. We are not eager to move on to the unknown. We want to rear our children and be able to hold our grandchildren. We want to finish the project we are working on, but when it is complete we suddenly have an idea for another one – just one more thing – always one more.

The gift that comes with a terminal diagnosis arrives in the form of having no time-frame to work within. You will eventually come to grips with the fact the second shoe will drop, but you no longer wait tensely for it to happen. You begin to adapt to living with short-term instead of long-term plans and you confirm that there are no certainties

9

in life. The sum total of these changes in lifestyle can be extremely liberating. Once acceptance takes place, time *no longer matters*. You accept that an enormous event is about to happen in your life and you are ready at all times.

As a result of my work, I am constantly being reminded that I am a terminal being. I sometimes find myself looking at a patient thinking, 'I could die before she does.' I am aware of how fragile and temporary life is, not just for those diagnosed with a terminal illness, but for every single one of us. Nevertheless, it is unlikely those who are not terminally diagnosed take their mortality as seriously as someone who has been terminally diagnosed does.

A terminal diagnosis should be taken seriously. However, all of us have heard of both miraculous healings and sudden, unexpected deaths. As far as life and death are concerned, I have learned that there are no sure things. I knew a woman who was given six months to live, but who refused to die until every one of her four children had graduated from college. Much to her doctor's surprise, she hung on for 16 years. I have also seen people pass a yearly check-up with flying colours and die the next week of a massive coronary. Because there are no sure things in life, we must all live every day to its fullest.

Balancing hope and practicality

When you receive a terminal diagnosis you must, of course, consider the facts, but it doesn't hurt to listen to your heart. Of course, every patient wants to believe they are the exception – the miracle case. Hope can work in your favour. However, it would be foolish to count on it. Check all the facts and settle down to live each day to the fullest. Be ready for a miracle, but don't rely on it exclusively. Get your affairs in order, but plan for either outcome.

The remaining time after a terminal diagnosis *can* be good. Each day takes on new meaning and importance when time is limited. Long-term plans now become short-term or are set aside entirely. Priorities change. Keeping the house clean becomes less important in the daily routine than sitting with a loved one watching the sky turn amber as the sun sets behind a mountain.

Pain and treatment

Often the fear of pain interferes with a peaceful existence. *Coming Home*, by Deborah Duda, addresses the issue of pain from an interesting standpoint. She writes that the greatest fear about death is physical pain and that people experience pain in different ways. It is a combination of physical feelings, emotional well-being, mental aspects and spiritual involvement. Pain serves a purpose. It is neither good nor bad; it's simply a messenger that tells us something in our body is not working properly. Therefore, patients need unique pain control programmes developed especially for them.

I am a migraine headache sufferer, so pain is no stranger in my life. My father also was a migraine sufferer. He experienced very little pain during his final illness and I often wonder if it was because he had learned how to deal with pain. Most migraine sufferers learn how to relax their bodies and not fight pain. They learn how to focus on something other than their pain to serve as a distraction. One of my favourite tricks is to place an ice bag on my throbbing temple and picture myself walking on a beach picking up interesting seashells. As I concentrate on the beach setting and the shells, I remove myself from the pain.

Don't suffer in silence

Most people are not accustomed to living with pain. The more foreign it is to a person, the more frightening it is. Do not fight your pain, but do not suffer in silence either. Let your carer or health professional know you hurt – no one will think you are 'weak'. They need to know so they can help you. Strive to get the greatest relief with the least amount of grogginess. Different drugs can be used together, alternated or given in different forms. Experiment under your doctor's direction to find the best treatment, with or without drugs, in your particular situation.

Addiction to medication

Hospice nurses feel strongly that addiction is not a concern. If addictive drugs are being used, they can be given in proportion to the severity of the pain. Consider them a necessity. Do not suffer with intense pain because of the fear of addiction! Pain relief is of utmost importance at this time. If the pain disappears, the addiction can be dealt with and reversed.

In spite of advancing technology in pain management patients do not always receive the pain relief that some would expect. I have found there is a gap in the education of healthcare professionals in dealing with hospice patients. Make sure you discuss any medication questions or concerns with your doctor or pharmacist and hospice team to make sure adequate pain control is maintained at all times.

Alternatives to medication

Look into alternative methods of pain relief that are gaining in popularity. There are pain control clinics, people who specialize in various methods of pain relief, and books written on the subject. Relaxation techniques, distraction and massage have all proven to be good ways to lessen pain.

Creative arts

An entirely new field using creativity for pain relief is evolving. Experimentation with creative arts is proving to be quite helpful for pain relief and is improving the quality of life for critically ill patients. *Thanatos* magazine (1991) defines creative arts as music, literature, dance, cassette tapes and poetry readings, as well as creative hobbies and recreational activities.

The variety of art disciplines that might be part of a creative arts programme depends on the strengths and resources of the carers and the patient. The most important objective of an arts programme is to diminish the impact of crisis created by terminal illness. Participation in an arts programme can improve the patient's quality of life and lower pain levels.

If you are housebound, watching television and thinking about your illness all day long, you are more likely to feel unproductive and depressed. Think about the tasks you previously enjoyed, or ones you never had time to pursue. Can any of these be done from bed or without leaving the house? You may want to take photographs or write poetry. You might choose to make a video or compose music. Each person has special creative talents. Now is the time to cultivate your creativity and make life more meaningful.

I watched an elderly gentleman paint with watercolours for the first time in his life. Every day he looked forward to moving from his bed to a card-table to paint. His pain decreased and his wife was less stressed because she saw him enjoying himself again.

His pictures had a muted, spiritual quality. He painted lighthouses and seascapes and his final step was to put a thin coat of white paint over the pictures, creating a unique, misty effect. He gave away the pictures to anyone who came to his home. His visitors coveted and treasured his pictures.

If you are interested in any creative avenues, check your phone book or ask your healthcare advisers to find out what is available in your area.

Medication precautions

In a hospital setting, medications are distributed and monitored routinely by the staff. A *Parents* magazine article (1991) quoted a study reported in the *Journal of the American Medical Association* which found that doctors in a large teaching hospital made on average two and a half errors every day in prescribing medication. Half of these errors were health-threatening to patients.

Ask questions about medication before taking it. When you are given a new prescription, ask the following questions before you collect it:

- What is the name of the medication?
- How does it work?
- What form (capsule, liquid) and strength is it?
- How often should it be taken?
- When should it be taken (with meals, before meals)?
- How long before you begin to see results?
- What are the possible side-effects?

If the medication does not seem to be working or does not agree with you, tell your doctor. When taking medication at home, follow the same precautions. Never swallow a pill or receive an injection without knowing what it is. If your doctor has not answered the questions to your satisfaction, ask the pharmacist so you can be fully informed before you begin to take a medication.

With most pain medication, it is important to keep a constant level in your body for it to be effective. Do not skip a dosage because you feel better! If you wait until you are experiencing pain, it will take added time for medication to reach the right level in your system to gain results.

Never mix medication from different pharmacies or doctors without checking with a medical professional. If the instructions say to take the medication on a full or empty stomach, follow these instructions as best you can. If you are unable to eat, and directions state to take it following a meal, take it with a cracker or glass of milk. Read all information that comes with a new prescription and heed all warnings.

Doctors assume a prescription is doing its job unless you tell them otherwise. If you experience unpleasant side-effects, notify your doctor. Doctors have no other way of finding out. Let your doctor know if the medicine is ineffective, your condition worsens after you have started the medication, or you build up a resistance to the medication. Everybody is different and medicines can have unusual effects. Suffering in silence helps no one. Express yourself! Giving doctors feedback means they can help you get the best results from the many drugs available.

Back rubs

A back rub can be relaxing and help you sleep. A soothing massage can ease aches and pains. Massage also helps prevent bedsores because it improves circulation. I like to warm lotion before applying it for a back rub. It makes my hands feel good and is not such a shock when it is applied. I either place the lotion container in hot water in a saucepan over low heat for a short time, or in the microwave for a few seconds. (Be extra cautious with plastic containers because they can melt.) Be sure to test the lotion on yourself before pouring it on the person.

Home remedies

In addition to prescription drugs, there are many helpful home remedies. Most families have their own favourite comforting tricks, which have been passed down from generation to generation. A hot-water bottle can soothe achy muscles or cramps, as can a heating pad. A cup of herbal tea to calm someone down, an ice pack on a throbbing head or a favourite music tape for distraction from pain can be successful 'medicines'. Make use of them!

Comfort

When I'm looking for a home remedy, I think back to the ways my mother made me feel better when I was a child. In the 1950s we had few drugs available, so mothers developed their own methods of treating ailments. My mother used to give me a spoonful of honey for a sore throat and chicken soup with homemade noodles for a head cold. She would tuck me into bed with one of my dad's giant white linen handkerchiefs under my pillow. It was comforting psychologically and I got well quickly. Today, when I get a cold, I stuff myself with cold-remedy tablets and never pause in my hectic daily activities. It takes me twice as long to get well and is not half as nice as being pampered.

14

Comfort is the key. When we are sick, we need to be comforted. Even your carer is comforted when he or she has made you feel better. Do not be afraid to ask for a heating pad or a back rub. Human contact is soothing for both the carer and you!

Cancer

Many patients with a terminal illness have cancer. Not because cancer is the number one cause of death – it actually ranks second to heart disease – but because, unlike heart disease, it usually gives a warning. Many of us know people who have died of cancer and we fear getting it.

Another mistaken fact about cancer is that it causes painful, agonizing deaths. Even advanced stages of cancer often inflict little or no pain. Statistics show that half of terminal cancer patients experience relatively little pain. Those who do have pain can control it well throughout the illness. My own father died of prostate cancer that had spread throughout his body. He never took anything stronger than aspirin and was quite comfortable with that.

Cancer information

Both the Imperial Cancer Research Fund and Macmillan Cancer Relief have a wealth of information available and are knowledgeable about numerous other resources in most communities. If possible, visit your local office or phone them and ask for printed material about your specific form of cancer.

If you are interested in being a part of an experimental programme or drug trial when all other treatment has proved ineffective ask your GP or local hospital for information.

The NHS has medical equipment available to lend to qualifying patients, available by referral through local surgeries. Enquire about volunteers, support groups, transportation to medical appointments and printed material. Some branches of the ICRF offer donated medical supplies or a wide range of wigs and cosmetic items to give you a lift. All these products are given free of charge.

Visit your local library, or have someone go for you, and check out any materials pertaining to your illness and health situation. Ask in your community for recommendations, check with any medical professionals and talk to people until you feel secure with the facts and are confident that everything possible is being done.

If you have a computer and can access the Internet, chat rooms are an innovative way to connect with other cancer patients to receive support and obtain information.

AIDS

Although there is no cure for AIDS, in 1982 the life expectancy after diagnosis was an average of only eight months. With recent research and new drug advances, the life expectancy of AIDS patients increases almost every year. Many AIDS patients remain in remission for years. In this section, I address only patients with advanced, acute AIDS.

AIDS information

People do not die from AIDS. AIDS is a virus that destroys the immune system and allows other diseases to infect the body. However, symptoms can be controlled, even in advanced cases, and comfort measures can be used to keep you as symptom- and pain-free as possible. The most common emotional reactions for AIDS patients to their illness are anxiety and fear, similar to those experienced by cancer patients.

Be well-informed. Read up on AIDS, find available resources in your community and look for a support group. Call accessible local rate numbers to find out where you can get help. It is important to research your choices before you become too sick to do so.

Only 2 per cent of AIDS patients spend their last days in hospitals. Most receive care in private homes, hospice units or special AIDS hospitals. As more knowledge is gained and shared, the fear that originally surrounded AIDS patients has lessened, and it continues to decrease. Support groups are also increasing so more and more AIDS patients are receiving excellent care and support.

Originally, misinformation about AIDS, its contagion, contraction and cure was common. Family support was often withheld, and patients were ashamed even to say the word 'AIDS'. It was bad enough to have a disease with no known cure, but many patients found they were shunned in addition. AIDS carried a stigma. Consequently, many AIDS patients died without the care cancer patients received.

In recent years, this stigma surrounding AIDS has decreased and more help is available to those needing it. Public grants are available to assist with financial matters, and support groups, volunteers, special hospice organizations and many other services are also available.

If you are an AIDS patient, you don't have to explain how you contracted the disease. Instead, let people know what is being done to slow down its progress and what they can do to assist you. Mend any broken family ties while you have the energy to do so. If you are unable to do this in person, you might write letters. This is not a time to hold grudges or allow loved ones to do likewise.

Hospital, home, hospice or convalescent care

It's important you are comfortable with the care you receive, whether it is at home, in a hospice unit or in the hospital. Before you make a single decision, check all the options available in your area. Gather available resource materials. Holders of private health insurance should enquire about possible time limits on benefits. Find out what is available in home-nursing care and from volunteer organizations.

You and your family should discuss the subject of where you wish to be cared for, especially if you wish to remain at home. When reaching a decision, everyone in the family needs to be honest about concerns and fears. Sometimes simply talking about the issues will resolve differences.

If you have trouble communicating your needs, you may be more comfortable in a hospital setting, being cared for by professionals rather than having family members feed and possibly assist with intimate tasks. If your illness requires care only a professional can administer adequately, skilled hospital care will be necessary and the choices will be more limited. Everyone involved must be satisfied with the decisions. Discuss all your options carefully before deciding.

But bear in mind, no decision has to be final. If you are in the hospital and decide you would rather be at home, you can ask to be discharged at any time and taken home by ambulance, if necessary. If you are an at-home hospice patient, you can be admitted to hospital if your needs change.

Hospital care or convalescent care

Hospital care and convalescent care are entirely different. Large general hospitals offer skilled care, while cottage hospitals and convalescent homes concentrate mainly on comfort measures. Skilled care is treatment that can be administered only by a medical person in a hospital setting. Certain treatments require special equipment that is available only in a hospital. Your care options will depend on your needs. When skilled care is not necessary, *acute-care hospitals* are required to discharge patients.

Advantages to hospital and convalescent care

A great advantage to both hospital care and convalescent care is that the family does not have to make as many major decisions about personal care. The patient is cared for routinely by professionals, emergencies are dealt with as they arise and doctor's visits are more frequent.

Another advantage to hospital care is that it frees other family members to fulfil their daily obligations. Often the primary carer is also the breadwinner in the family, and it is impossible for him or her to stay at home and care for the patient.

Visitors

One distinct disadvantage for hospital patients is that it is more difficult to screen visitors. Uninterrupted rest is often impossible. And it is not always possible for the family to spend private time with their loved one. The nursing staff has duties to perform and often they cannot accommodate the patient's need for privacy.

For instance, one day I was trying to have a serious conversation with an acutely ill friend while the cleaner mopped the floor and whistled a happy tune. It was distracting and I finally gave up in despair. Likewise there may be times when you don't feel like having visitors, but you don't have a good way to keep people out of your hospital room. The time I did see a 'Do not disturb' sign on a closed door, nobody was paying much attention to it.

Hospital know-how

Depending on the situation, pain control may be better or worse in a hospital setting. If the staff are overworked or short-handed medication may not be distributed on time. However, if injections or drips are required, the staff are better equipped to handle these. Oxygen is easily available. Doctors, nurses and medical staff can ease the burden on family members who are trying to make difficult decisions.

It is also easier to maintain cleanliness in a hospital where the professionals know the right way to change a bed with a patient in it and give thorough sponge baths. Bedsores are more easily prevented due to nurses' general know-how. In the hospital, when a pressure sore begins, it is treated immediately, before it becomes unmanageable.

Hospice-care units

Hospice-care units are excellent choices for people who prefer the hospice philosophy (see page 21) but have no full-time carer to administer at-home hospice care. To find a hospice unit, check your local phone book, ask your GP or local hospital, or log on to the Internet. For hospice care for AIDS, call the National AIDS Helpline, which is free and available 24 hours a day, seven days a week, on 0800 567 123; or the Terrence Higgins Trust Helpline, available 12 noon to 10 p.m. 365 days a year, on 020 742 1010. If you are in London, try the London Lighthouse Information Service on 0208 383 5647. (See page 123 for more information.)

Home care

For the patient to remain at home for the duration of the illness, one person needs to be able to devote themselves full-time to the patient's care, 24 hours a day. This person becomes what we call the primary carer. In situations where no primary carer is available, the job may be shared or done in shifts.

Tell your family or carer if you want to be cared for at home. If you have a private health insurance policy, see what is available in home care; ask your family and friends if they are willing to work out a schedule of care for you.

Involve a hospice organization

At-home care is easiest if a hospice is involved. They educate carers in health measures that make care easier and of better quality. Health insurance often covers the expense of home-nursing visits or hospice care. Some life insurance companies allow benefits to be paid prior to death so the money can be used to cover care during a terminal illness. Some health insurance policies have special provisions for long-term care. Investigate all your options to make sure you are using your insurance coverage to best advantage.

Loved ones close by

The most positive reason for home care is that the atmosphere is more relaxed and casual. Rigid schedules are unnecessary and the patient can remain in familiar surroundings. People often feel better in their own homes. At home, loved ones can be actively involved in the patient's well-being, which can be extremely rewarding for all concerned.

In your own home, you can set the rules and regulations. Your pets can sleep on the hospital bed, and so can your spouse; you can stay up all night and catnap during the day. If you feel up to it, you can get out of bed and take a walk outside; if not, you can snuggle up with a good book. Experiment and use your imagination. This is *your* time. There are no ground rules or guidelines. The possibilities are unlimited, and the choices are yours.

Benefits of home-hospice care

I have observed many home-hospice cases and have been involved in the care of several of my own loved ones. I can vouch that the period of grieving is greatly decreased for those who have had the pleasure of taking care of their loved ones. My mother and I received frequent daily rewards while caring for Dad that left us with lasting memories and eased our grief. Seven years later, when my mother was in her final illness, I was able to spend almost a month with her. We had midnight snacks of milk and cookies as I sat on her bed and talked. Those precious memories will be with me for ever.

Proper equipment

If you choose to stay at home, look into equipment that can make you more comfortable and make the job easier for your carer. Talk to a hospital equipment supplier and explain your needs. They are listed in the Yellow Pages under 'Hospital Services and Supplies', 'Medical Equipment', or 'Hospices'. Ask if they can recommend items for your particular situation.

If and when it becomes too difficult to get to a bathroom, a bedside commode is extremely useful. Also available are bedside tables and trays, walkers, wheelchairs, bedpans, urinals and equipment for lifting or for increased safety. Rails can be installed near the shower or bath and the toilet can be raised with a doughnut-like seat. Other special devices include shower seats, hospital beds, humidifiers, vaporizers, fans, air-flotation pads for mattresses to help prevent bed sores and special 'egg crate' mattress pads. Medical equipment gives your carer extra help, conserves energy and makes you more comfortable.

Homemade help

When ready-made products don't offer solutions, use your imagination to solve problems. I have seen home remedies work wonders, such as homemade, specially shaped pillows to place in extra-sensitive spots, perhaps between the knees or under a sore arm. I have seen a toilet seat wrapped with foam to protect a tender tailbone. I have seen pieces of fake fur wrapped around limbs, and beds filled with pillows to prop patients in a comfortable position.

All you and your carer need is a little imagination to accomplish great things. Do not assume a solution is impossible until you have exhausted every possible source. Friends love to be asked for suggestions to find an innovative solution. Don't be embarrassed to ask them for help with a tricky problem.

Hospices

The word 'hospice' is derived from the Latin root word *hospes*, which means 'the mutual caring of people for each other'. The modern words 'hostel', 'hospital' and 'hospitality' were derived from *hospes*. In times past, a hostel was a place where travellers were lodged, cherished and refreshed. 'Hospice' stands for an entire philosophy of life and death where people who are incurably ill can be tenderly cared for as they travel to the end of this life.

A hospice is similar to an acute-care hospital. It has nurses and staff on duty. Hospices are sometimes houses or buildings near, but separate from, acute-care hospitals. Loved ones have freedom to visit and may even stay overnight. No curative or heroic measures are used. Like home-hospice care, pain control and comfort are the main priorities of hospices.

Hospice philosophy

The hospice philosophy emphasizes comfort, communication and peace. The main purpose is to assist the patient in the passage from this life to the next in a natural, peaceful manner, free from pain and stress in a serene environment. Hospice care is usually provided in a patient's private home or in a special hospice. Either way, the hospice philosophy is the same. Recently, some acute-care hospitals have begun to offer hospice-like care.

The hospice theory stresses *quality* of life rather than *quantity*. The main goal of hospice is to allow a patient to die with dignity, freedom and self-respect, with as little pain as possible, unafraid, at peace and among friends. Hospice care ministers to the family as a whole, as well as the patient. There are a number of helpful books about hospice care. (See the reading list on page 118.)

Home-hospice care

To die at home is to die surrounded with love in a familiar setting. Many people who are taken home to die find less need for pain relief because of the relaxed schedule and familiar surroundings.

An important factor in choosing home-hospice care is whether there is a hospice outreach organization covering your area or if there is a hospice nearby. With hospice outreach, the family has support throughout the illness. Hospice teams help with care, but more important, they teach the family or carers how to make their job simpler. They can advise on equipment, give baths, change dressings, do professional chores and offer emotional support. They have a doctor on call, as well as a spiritual adviser. Many have a nutritionist and physical therapist on duty as well.

Hospice volunteers

Hospice organizations have volunteers who act as family friends and provide respite care, run errands or just sit and listen to you talk. Hospice volunteers are trained and experienced in dealing with all aspects of terminal illness and death. They often act as the go-between for family members when difficult matters need to be discussed. They arrive with compassion, not pity; knowledge instead of fear; and with experience in making you comfortable. They encourage communication about all aspects of home care and dying at home, and can serve as guides in unfamiliar territory.

It is possible to choose home-hospice care without the backing of a hospice organization, but it is not as easy.

Resuscitate or no-code instructions

Once the decision is made for either home care or institutional care, the next matter to be discussed should be resuscitation and life-support equipment. If you desire no heroic measures of resuscitation, artificial feeding or hydration (keeping up your fluid intake), these wishes need to be spelt out legally in a detailed document called an 'advance directive' or 'living will'. Leave nothing to chance! It is important to spell out each detail. Your consultant can advise you about this paperwork.

When everyone is in agreement, you need to sign the proper papers and your doctor needs to be informed and given copies of the paperwork.

A few phone calls should be all it takes to obtain the information. Begin by enquiring at a hospice organization, if there is one, or at a local hospital. Anyone who deals with emergency health situations should have the current information, such as paramedics, A and E departments or even the staff at a local doctor's surgery.

In case of medical emergency

If you have decided on home care, find out what happens in case of a medical emergency. Paramedics are required to administer resuscitation measures, even if family members tell them it is not the patient's wish.

Local hospice organizations can advise you. If you are not using a hospice organization, check with your county or city council, or the local coroner's office about rescue efforts. Pick up your telephone and play detective until you have tracked down someone who can give you the answers you need.

Physical needs

If you choose home care, you and your carers need to be aware of the special needs that arise with a terminal illness. Even if you are hospitalized, it is wise to be aware of how well these needs are being met.

Nutrition

Depending on the progression of your illness, your body may no longer require or desire nourishment. In this case, it would be foolish to make yourself eat a certain number of calories at each meal. Liquids are necessary, but food is not. The human body is a remarkable machine. It lets you know what it needs.

If you have no desire for food, don't force yourself to eat. Often just smelling an orange or eating one bite of a favourite food is all you need to feel satisfied. At home or in hospital, follow whatever feels right. Naturally, if you are able to eat, you will feel stronger and more emotionally stable.

Follow your cravings

I have seen many ill people feel compelled to eat, fighting nausea, simply to please loved ones. Do not get into that cycle; follow your cravings instead. What harm can it do if you have ice cream for breakfast, an orange for lunch and pizza for dinner? If some days your stomach is rebelling against vegetables or meat, it is no big deal. Maybe tomorrow you will crave nothing but a big green salad.

Additional nutrition

If you wish to take in more nutrition but have no appetite, look for some of the many nutritional drinks on the market. They are similar to milk shakes and are often more appealing than solid food. These drinks come in various flavours and can be purchased in chemists and most food shops. People tell me they also freeze the drinks. This makes them similar to ice cream and that is more palatable to some people. Let your body be your guide, and go with whatever feels right for you.

Dehydration

You do have to keep up your fluid intake or you will become dehydrated. Most people continue to desire liquids even when they have no appetite for food. As long as you can swallow, drink as much liquid as possible. If it is difficult for you to drink water, ice cubes or frozen juice cubes can suffice. Frequent small sips may serve you better than big gulps. Carbonated drinks may cause gas in an empty stomach, and so may drinking through a straw. If gas is a problem, switch to fruit drinks instead.

Many patients I have known liked cold foods best, such as frozen juice bars, ice cream and frozen yogurt. Let your carers and friends know what you prefer. They are probably waiting with bated breath to serve you some delectable treat. Even if you can only sniff the aroma or eat one bite, it gives those supplying you with a titbit of pleasure. Don't deny them that personal reward.

Favourite foods

Although my dad had little appetite during his final illness, he would occasionally surprise us with a request for something specific. Strawberries were one of his favourite foods, and one day he told us he had a taste for them.

It was early March and strawberries were not easy to find at the market. However, one morning I was fortunate enough to find some rather puny-looking ones. I took my treasure home and prepared the best-looking strawberry in the basket. I removed the stem and set it in the centre of a fancy sherbet dish. Then I carried it to him on a silver tray. How Dad's eyes lit up when he saw that single strawberry!

Much to my delight, he savoured the smell, the feel and the taste of it. He smacked his lips and rubbed his belly as he swallowed it. That single strawberry gave us both great pleasure. To this day, I never prepare strawberries without thinking about Dad.

Even if you can no longer eat full meals, you can still share mealtimes with your family. I have seen families take meals into their loved one's rooms even when they no longer had an appetite. Share in the dinnertime conversation and have a time of fellowship as long as the aroma of food does not nauseate you and family members are not bothered by the fact that you are not eating.

Reassure your family that you enjoy simply being with them and watching them eat. Possibly play with a bowl of flavoured jelly or sip your drink along with them to help them feel comfortable about eating in front of you. It can be a nice time of sharing, with physical nourishment being secondary.

Elimination

When food intake is decreased, bowel movements become irregular or sluggish. This is not a major concern unless it makes you uncomfortable. Many people expect to have a daily bowel movement, and any change in routine is upsetting. As long as you feel comfortable, don't be alarmed. Let your doctor or nurse know if you have any discomfort or bloating. Many good remedies on the market can relieve discomfort. However, do not self-treat with over-the-counter remedies until you have checked with your healthcare team. In case of diarrhoea, seek medical care immediately. Dehydration from diarrhoea can occur rapidly in a person with unstable health.

When you are no longer able to manage trips to the bathroom by yourself, look into other options. Open communication with your carer is necessary. If you want to be helped on to a bedside commode and then left alone until you are finished, say so. Be sure toilet paper is left within your reach. Ask to have the door closed or sheet placed over your lap. This is one of the most delicate and difficult issues for patients and their families to approach. Sensitive communication makes it less embarrassing for everyone. Appreciate the assistance from your carers. Remember, you would do the same for them.

Undergarments

Disposable undergarments, similar to disposable nappies, are necessary sometimes. They come in many different sizes and styles. Experiment to find the most suitable one for you. Loss of bladder control and having to be 'changed' can be distressing. However, if you and your carer handle it gently and openly, the awkwardness need not last long. Cleanliness is easier to maintain when disposable undergarments are used, and it takes care of the difficult issue of getting a patient out of bed and into a bathroom.

Honest, open discussion that comes straight from the heart can prevent daily embarrassment. Each family will handle these personal care situations in the manner that works for their own family.

The first time I changed my mother's underclothing, she began to cry. 'Nobody should ever have to do this,' she said. I stopped what I was doing and looked into her eyes. 'Mom, how many nappies of mine did you change? You did it without thinking about it and because you loved me, right? Now it's my turn and I want to do this because I love you. Please don't be embarrassed or let it make you feel sad. Just allow me to care for you like you cared for me, OK?' I dried her eyes and smiled at her. 'You're such a good daughter,' she told me. That was a moment I treasure to this day. She gave me a gift by permitting me to care for her and by her simply appreciating the nature in which it was given.

Relaxation

Relaxation is very important for your peace of mind. You can learn to relax in a number of ways, whether you are in the hospital or at home. Think of ways your senses can soothe and relax you. What kind of smells, sounds or touch would help you sleep or just relax? For example,

- Ask your carer to give you a back rub
- Listen to relaxing music
- Ease emotional stress with aromatherapy

Bed placement

When the time comes to be confined to bed, locate the bed in the most suitable spot. Don't automatically think you have to be in your regular bedroom. With home-hospice patients, a hospital bed is usually set up in a central location so the patient can still be part of the family. Living rooms work well, and so do dining rooms or family rooms.

Place the bed in a light, cheerful spot where there is room for chairs around it. Don't worry about being a successful interior decorator at this point – the bed can even be placed in the centre of the room. Ask for bed sheets in your favourite colour or design – forget plain white ones! If you have special pictures or knick-knacks you want to see, move them into your new 'bedroom'. You might want a television, a vapourizer, an oscillating fan or a laptop computer nearby, depending on what makes you feel most comfortable.

Be comfortable

Wear pyjamas, a tracksuit or even your favourite jeans. Now is the time to be a nonconformist and do what makes *you* feel best. Many men grow beards at this point because they dislike being shaved in bed. Find a hairdresser or barber who can come to the house to keep your hair styled. Nothing lifts the spirit like a fresh haircut. If you don't have a regular hairstylist who makes house calls, contact a local beauty college. Ask that they put a card on the bulletin board requesting someone to come to your home.

Draw on all the senses. Do not forget the pleasure of smell. Aromatherapy uses different scents to help people relax. Take advantage of relaxing fragrances such as lavender or mimosa. Soothe your emotions with pleasant scents of vanilla or cinnamon, which evoke happy childhood memories for many people. Splash on your favourite cologne or aftershave. Place scented candles, a spice ball or a bowl of potpourri in your room. Lovely smells can give both you and your carer a real lift.

Sexuality and intimacy

A person's sexuality does not come to an end with a terminal diagnosis. It is still natural to want to be held and touched and to continue intimate relationships.

If your illness is contagious, be sure you know all the ways in which it can be transmitted, and relay those facts to loved ones. If you are not contagious, but have unfamiliar medical equipment hooked up, explain the equipment to others. Remember that an IV line may be threatening to someone who has never seen one before. (A permanent IV line is inserted under the skin in the chest, and leaves a small bulge.) Explain to your family and visitors any unusual bulges or unfamiliar medical equipment that is attached to your body. Let people know if you have any tender area they need to avoid touching. As a knowledgeable patient, you can ease those fears. Some people may be afraid of causing you unnecessary pain or dislodging medical equipment by jostling you.

Touch

If you are in a hospital bed, ask that the sides be let down so people can get closer. Let visitors know if you want to hold their hand or receive a kiss. Most people do not do these things without an invitation. They worry about invading your privacy, and need to know you don't mind. If you are unsteady or if you might fall out of bed, remind visitors to pull up the sides again before they leave.

Touching is important for both patient and visitor. I had a precious experience with my aunt as she lay dying. She reached for my hand and I warned her that my hands were unusually cold. As she took my hand and kissed it, she said, 'A cold hand is lots better to hold than no hand at all.' I let her hold my icy hand for as long as she needed.

Unless you have to be careful about contact because of impaired

27

immunities, ask for hugs when you need them! Again, people often hesitate because they worry about hurting you or dislodging medical equipment. Hugs are good for both you and your visitors. Put a sign over your bed that says, 'I need hugs! Please comply.'

Ask visitors to apply lip balm on your dry lips, get a fresh jug of water or plump up your pillows. Do not hesitate to ask! It makes the visitor feel good to help and also makes you more comfortable. Everyone likes to be useful and they are grateful to fulfil your requests. I always ask what I can do when I visit someone who is ill. If nothing is needed, I feel a bit dejected afterwards. Do not deny people the pleasure of helping you.

Sexual contact

Assuming you have addressed the issue of contagion, sexual contact can continue. Communication and honesty are especially necessary. Touching, embracing and kissing are all joyful experiences you don't have to give up. Put your imagination to good use, use common sense and talk to your partner about your desire for physical contact.

Spontaneous sexual activity is probably no longer possible, so timing is vitally important. Plan private times when you feel the most comfortable and when your medication is working most effectively. Explore new ways to be intimate with your partner.

In addition to the enjoyment of sexual activity, the release of sexual energy can reduce stress and promote more peaceful relationships. If you notice a marked change in your libido, sexual response or functioning, check with a medical professional. Illness, treatment or medication often have a direct effect on these responses. Find someone you feel comfortable discussing personal matters with and do not assume you have to set your sex life aside.

Let your loved one know it is still all right to cuddle under the covers, and to enjoy each other's bodies. Be open and honest about any feelings of unattractiveness you may be experiencing due to weight loss, surgery or treatment. We are usually our own worst critics and our loved ones do not even see these 'defects'. Love has a depth that goes beyond superficial beauty. Think about how you would feel towards your loved one if the tables were turned.

Humour

A little humour goes a long way. Laugh at yourself and keep the atmosphere light about any physical changes if you can. Set the pace for your loved ones so that all of you can be open about the changes while you learn to accept them.

When comedienne Gilda Radner was battling ovarian cancer, I was surprised to see so many pictures of her displayed in magazines. Usually people who have been in the public eye are concerned about their appearance. Yet Gilda was being photographed with very little hair and toothpick-thin arms and legs, with dark circles under her eyes, grinning impishly for the camera. I was touched and impressed by her courage. It was only later, when I read an article about her husband Gene Wilder, that I came to truly understand the situation.

Gene Wilder told *People* magazine (1991) that after Gilda completed a series of chemotherapy she lost most of her hair. He said, 'When her hair fell out, she was devastated, but eventually she made jokes about that too . . . those little bean sprouts growing on top of her head were adorable, like a newborn baby. I thought it was sexy.'

Being able to call the fine hair on Gilda's head 'bean sprouts' made them cute rather than distressing. Because Gilda's husband thought she was 'sexy', she was also able to accept her changed appearance. A situation like losing her hair could have been devastating to Gilda; instead, it was something to joke about because her husband accepted it. When *you* are comfortable with your looks, it frees others to feel the same way.

Romance

In addition to accepting your physical appearance, add some romance to your life. The Wilsons are a good example of how a small change in atmosphere can improve the lives of housebound people.

I always looked forward to my visits with Lois and Joe Wilson. When her husband became ill, Lois set up the hospital bed in the family room right next to a large stone fireplace. It was a comfortable setting for Joe to spend his final days. One chilly, rainy day, I curiously asked if they ever had a fire in the fireplace. Lois was so caught up in Joe's physical care that this possibility never entered her mind. My remark jogged their memories just as I hoped it would.

On my next visit, I was pleased to see a crackling, blazing fire. After looking at the fire, I inquired about Joe's favourite music. They took the hint and the next time I visited there was soft music playing. With a little more prodding, they were spending romantic times in front of a warm fire, sipping fruit juice and listening to soft music.

These special, quiet times can be considered gifts – especially when you have more free time than you did before your illness. Live each moment to the fullest!

2
Emotional adjustments

In addition to the physical changes that take place during a major illness come a wide array of emotional adjustments.

Emotions in turmoil

Anger, depression, yearning, guilt, fear and sadness usually follow the initial responses of shock and denial to a terminal diagnosis. These feelings can arrive at any time, and they fluctuate.

Dr Elisabeth Kübler-Ross was the first person to document the feelings experienced by dying patients. Her research opened many doors to a subject that previously had been tightly locked. Dr Elisabeth Kübler-Ross feels that only when people are able to accept death as a part of life are they able to make the transition peacefully. She also feels that the most precious times in a person's life come only after they realize they are finite beings.

She writes in *Death: The Final Stage of Growth* that when people do not accept death, they live in denial and their lives can be empty and without purpose. With the acceptance of mortality comes the opportunity to make life more meaningful. Tuck this thought into your toolbox for repairs on bad days as you prepare your heart for wisdom.

Anger

Anger is a common reaction after shock and denial. You may ask, 'Why me?' You may be angry because you feel powerless and unable to control the course your life has taken. You may be angry because it seems as if all your careful plans have fallen apart, and you have been treated unfairly. You may feel like a pressure cooker full of emotion ready to blow its lid.

Some people direct their anger at their loved ones or at themselves. They may blame God for dealing them a losing hand. Being angry at God can be frightening. However, I personally feel God understands when people become angry.

Expressing your anger

If you are experiencing anger, try actively to remove it. Find constructive ways to work out your anger so that it doesn't erupt unexpectedly and harmfully. I know a young child, wise beyond his years, who told me that because our heads are round, anger just swims around and around inside, and cannot get out. He came up with two ways to get anger out of his head. One was through his mouth, that is, by talking about his angry feelings. The other was through his hand, by writing down his feelings. Talking about or writing down anger are excellent ways to work it out. This young man's mother gave him a tape recorder so he could express his anger on tape. It helped him tremendously.

Write about your anger in a notebook. No one needs to see what you have written. The important part is to put it down on paper and get it out of your system. Write fast and furiously until you feel calmer.

Another constructive way to vent anger is to find a trusted friend, support group, pastor or counsellor, and talk to them about your angry feelings. As you express your anger, it slowly eases out of your life. If you simply ignore or repress the angry feelings, on the other hand, they may explode in hurtful, damaging ways at inappropriate times or at innocent people.

Physical exercise

If you are able to participate in physical activities, work out your angry feelings with exercise. Pound a pillow or hit a tennis ball against a wall. Go for a brisk walk or sing along with a lively song with the volume turned all the way up. Do anything you can to release your anger – do not let fury seethe inside you.

Depression

Depression is a growing problem in an increasingly stressful world. One out of every five British people and one out of eight Americans is treated for depression during his or her lifetime. Every year millions of people are depressed to the extent they cannot function effectively and must seek some kind of treatment.

If depression is so prevalent in healthy people, is it any wonder it plays a major role with a person already weakened by illness? The first important step is to identify the signs of depression. Until the problem has an identity, it cannot be addressed. Depression is normal in a person who is critically ill. Overwhelming sadness over missed opportunities is natural. After depression is recognized, steps can be taken to deal with it. Left unacknowledged, depression can grow to immense proportions and take over your life.

Cleansing tears

Don't confuse shedding tears with depression. Crying is a way to relieve tension and sadness, and to express what words cannot. Don't be ashamed or embarrassed when you cry. Tears lower your body's stress level and have a relaxing effect. If your crying makes your loved ones uncomfortable, explain why you're crying. Children, especially, feel they are to blame when adults cry. Reassure them your tears are over the situation and not the result of anything they did. You might tell them about the old Yiddish saying, 'What soap is to the body, tears are to the soul.'

When you allow your tears to flow, you give others permission to comfort you. While they comfort you, they are also soothed. To cry alone can be refreshing, but it denies you the added comfort and solace from others. If your sobbing becomes uncontrollable or you feel overwhelmed by depression or suicidal thoughts, seek professional help.

Depression can be the result of the disease itself or a side-effect of treatment or medication. If you are overcome with despair, talk it over with your healthcare team to see if it is physiological. If it is, deal with it from that standpoint. If not, use the same methods of processing depression as you would anger – talk or write about it. It is a good idea to talk over your feelings with loved ones. Finally, try not to spend too much time alone when you are depressed.

Other suggestions

Often depression is the result of anger and repressed emotions. If you do not already have a strong support system, search for one in the form of friends, family or a support group. Find an unbiased listener who lets you express yourself, talk about your sadness and admit to your despair. Once you have organized your thoughts and identified the reason for your sadness, do not dwell on the negative aspects. Listen to your feelings and turn them into positives. Find the things that make you feel better about your life. For example, make a list of what you are still capable of doing rather than what you can no longer do.

Perfectionism

I have observed that perfectionism and depression are like Siamese twins – extremely difficult to separate. Perfectionists do constant battle with depression because they can never live up to their own unreasonably high expectations. When perfectionists become ill, it is double trouble. They expect the body to function perfectly, and it no longer does. Not only is the body imperfect, but now the person can no longer perform as well as she or he wishes. Perfectionists need to accept that humans are imperfect beings. You need to love yourself in your imperfect state. Life holds very little quality without self-acceptance.

Helpful tip

The way you carry yourself can lift your spirits or drag you down. Watch the way you sit and stand. Do your shoulders droop in a defeated attitude? Strive to improve your physical demeanour. When you square your shoulders and lift your chin, you feel better about yourself. Pretend you feel great for a few minutes at a time and pretty soon you will begin to believe it!

Be gentle with yourself

Treat yourself gently when you are feeling down. It's not selfish to be good to yourself. It helps your mental attitude, and can often alleviate physical symptoms. It is all right to pamper yourself with sweet-smelling perfume, a bouquet of flowers or a new pair of pyjamas. Even if you are confined to your home or bed, you can still find ways to indulge yourself. Ask friends to help, if need be. Splurge on a book you want to read or a delicious dessert. After you have catered to yourself a bit, it's time to lower your expectations and listen to yourself.

Self-talk

Whether you realize it or not, you talk to yourself all day long. You give yourself instructions, 'Now let's get out of bed.' You give yourself either praise or criticism. For some unknown reason, most of us believe what we hear. Many of our mistaken ideas come from false self-talk.

To see if negative self-talk is a problem for you, make an effort to listen to what you are saying to yourself for the next few days. Pay special attention to negative thoughts. Make a concentrated effort to rid yourself of degrading, negative or melancholy statements. Turn these statements into positives and speak kindly to yourself.

Begin early in the morning by telling yourself you are going to have a good day. Look in the mirror and announce that you are feeling better, whether you are or not. Smile and say, 'I am a worthy individual, even though I may not be as productive as I used to be.' Talk to yourself as you would a well-loved friend, not an enemy. When I pay close attention to my own self-talk, I notice I say things to myself I would never think of saying to another human being. My favourite derogatory statement is to call myself stupid. 'How can you be so stupid?' I ask myself frequently during the day. I would never call anyone else stupid, but I do it repeatedly to myself in my internal dialogue.

As you listen to your own self-talk, begin to change it so it no longer damages your self-worth. People who are in poor health need a generous amount of affection. Start by giving it to yourself.

Yearning

Along with negative self-talk, a feeling of yearning often accompanies depression. With any incurable illness comes a natural feeling of yearning – you may yearn for time that was seemingly wasted, for good health that was not appreciated, for all the things left undone that may no longer be possible. Or you may yearn for the plans you had for the future, which may no longer be feasible.

Following a terminal diagnosis, your priorities change and possibly your roles change as well. Some plans have to be postponed, some changed and some cancelled. To yearn for unfulfilled dreams is natural, but it can also waste valuable time.

I observed this in a patient named Alice. Alice had reared a large family, all the time putting aside her desire to write a novel. At last her youngest child left for college and Alice began to place on paper the words that had been forming in her head for years. She had completed the first two chapters when she became ill. She spent the next four months recovering from surgery, which was followed up by radiation treatments, all the time hoping to stall the progress of the disease long enough so she could regain her strength and finish her book.

I met her following her radiation treatments. Not only was Alice in a deep depression, but she was also filled with bitterness and rage. You could feel the despair when you entered her home. Her children eventually stopped coming round, neighbours stopped visiting and her husband spent most of his time outdoors working in the garden. Alice talked of nothing but her unfinished book, yet she was never able to get back to her typewriter.

She died isolated by disappointment and shattered dreams. An obsession over her thwarted goal took precedence over a home filled with love and laughter. If she had concentrated on the love of friends and family instead of hanging on to her unrealized dream, her life might have been totally different.

Determine your goals

Each of us sets the scene around us. Have you set the scene to your life's 'play' in a way that encourages and inspires friendship and love, or in a way that drives these things away? What do you yearn for? Have you arranged an appropriate environment for your dream to come true? Spend some time in thought to determine your immediate goals. If it is easier to clarify your thoughts on paper, write down your goals as you reach decisions.

Live in the moment

A good way to relieve yearning is to live one day at a time, without looking too far into the past or too far into the future. Consider the way children live. Children recognize this gift of present-time. They don't worry about the past and they don't put all their hopes in the future. It is a good way to live, for there is no certainty for any of us except in the present. Make the most of today and don't waste precious moments wishing for what cannot be.

Guilt

Guilt is easy to recognize because it starts with the phrases, 'If only', 'I should have' and 'Why didn't I?' Guilt is perfectly natural and understandable, but it wastes valuable time and energy during an illness when both may be in short supply. Listen to statements you may make that begin with these three phrases, stop yourself and then take the time to rephrase them. Learn to turn them into positive statements that encourage rather than discourage you.

Overcome negativity

I once visited a man who had every reason to feel guilty. His lifestyle had been less than healthy and now, at barely 40, he was in the final stages of lung cancer. Ben had been a heavy smoker for most of his life and had abused his body with drugs, poor nutrition and lack of exercise.

I had glanced at Ben's chart before leaving the office and saw the cancerous tumour in his body had wrapped around his spine. During surgery, his spinal cord had been cut, so he was paralysed from the waist down. His situation looked extremely discouraging on paper, and I approached his home with a heavy heart.

A radiant young woman who was very pregnant answered the door. I assumed it was Ben's daughter. Instead, Sally turned out to be Ben's wife; she was expecting their first child.

I was pleasantly surprised when I met Ben. His eyes sparkled in spite of his condition. As we talked, Sally climbed awkwardly on to the hospital bed to be closer to Ben. The love, joy and kindness of this remarkable couple instantly warmed me. After we got better acquainted, I couldn't help but ask how they had overcome all the negative aspects of Ben's condition.

'Heck,' Ben said in a heavy Southern drawl, 'who has time to be complaining? I know the odds are against me right now, but Sally and I don't have any time to waste on fussing. We're enjoying whatever time we have.'

I went home smiling, feeling as if I had seen a real-life miracle. Smokers who contract lung cancer often feel guilty. It takes a special kind of person to accept what is and not wallow in guilt. The past cannot be changed, and neither could the future in this case. They had only the present moment to live and they were doing just that.

If you are plagued by guilt, release it. You might write down your feelings on paper, then tear the paper to shreds or burn it as a symbol of riddance. Or talk about your guilt with a person you trust and work it out that way. Don't let guilty feelings get the best of you. They are corrosive to your spirit. Guilt is your enemy!

A *unique experience*

Death is unknown. We only die once and nobody can tell us what it is like. Doing anything for the first time is frightening. Having to do it with nobody to tell us exactly what it is like makes it even more so. When I was expecting my first baby, I wanted and needed to hear every woman's story about childbirth. It was reassuring to hear about their experiences. However, when the time came for my baby to be born, it wasn't like any experience I had heard about. It was a unique experience, like nobody else's. I believe death will be the same way.

A patient once told me that he felt more prepared for death than for the dying process. He believed death would be similar to the relocation he had done many times in his life as he moved about the country with his job. This young man hated losing physical control and having to depend upon others for his care. The loss of independence frightened him. He didn't want to be a burden and had no guarantees he would not become one before his death.

He talked extensively about 'cleaning house'. He was cleaning both his physical house and his emotional one, straightening out matters and putting everything in order. He did not want to leave any unfinished business.

Research shows that writing and talking are successful ways to clean your emotional house. They are the two best antidotes to 'leaving your house in disarray'. If you do not feel comfortable discussing soul-wrenching feelings, write them down. When you see your emotions written on a piece of paper, they won't appear as insurmountable.

Death – a transition

I have been with many terminally ill people when they died. Not one of these people struggled against death or fought it. They willingly moved out of their bodies, making a smooth transition. They all left a feeling of peace, with a touch of joy, in the room behind them. It was obvious to me that only the body had died, not the person.

Our present bodies are the only ones we have ever had, so we are understandably attached to them. I have noticed that as death approaches, people seem to become aware that the present body is weak and prone to disease, aches and pains. They become less enchanted with it. They seem to realize that the body is not really who they are; instead, it is seen as a temporary dwelling place.

When I look at a fuzzy caterpillar, I have to smile at the ingenuity of their creation. I feel certain that one reason they exist is so that writers will have an analogy to use about life, death, our present bodies and our eternal bodies. The comparison may be overused and overworked, but it remains the clearest way to explain life after death.

A caterpillar begins its life contentedly crawling about. Then one day it has to give up its peaceful life, the only life it has ever known. It has to give up the furry little body that it was perfectly content with up to this point. It does so effortlessly and without a struggle.

Each spring when my children were young, we would capture a caterpillar and watch the progress. We would put the caterpillar in an empty jar and watch as it attached itself to the lid and became immobile. Within a couple of days, the process was complete. The caterpillar was no longer visible. Instead, all that remained, attached to the lid of the jar, was a dried, dead-looking shell. But, pretty soon the shell moved! Then we removed the lid from the jar and put it outside so when the process was complete, the beautiful butterfly could fly away.

As the butterfly fought its way out of the cocoon, it flapped its wings repeatedly. I was told never to help the butterfly by freeing it prematurely. The struggle it was going through was necessary to dry and strengthen its wings. To help would interrupt this important process and the butterfly would be unable to fly. The struggle served a valuable purpose, though not an obvious one.

Soon the butterfly would be free and my children and I would watch as it took off, reaching heights that were never possible to the caterpillar. A butterfly can reach the top of a tree effortlessly and quickly; it can catch a wind current and drift about. Its new, improved body is not only much more useful, but also exquisitely beautiful. How can a fuzzy, brown creature turn into an orange, yellow and black mosaic design? We cannot tell, just as we cannot tell what kind of creature we will become after our metamorphosis.

If, on the other hand, your fears seem to be centred on the question of life after death, rather than on the process of dying or of leaving loved ones behind, consult a pastor or a trusted friend. Express your fears and seek help in finding answers to any specific questions.

One day at a time

The time remaining may be mere weeks, it may be months or it may be years. Live each day – actually each moment – to the fullest without worrying about tomorrow. I believe prayer helps. Pray about anything and everything. Praying with your loved ones can be soothing and enrich your family bond.

Begin and end each day in a reverent way, either alone or with your loved ones. Spending quiet time in thought increases wisdom. Allow yourself the gift of solitude and reflection. At this time, be sure to emphasize the quality of life rather than quantity.

Do whatever you feel up to doing on each particular day. Do not force yourself to accomplish great feats, but do not coddle yourself either! Enjoy warm sunshine on your face or the smell of a freshly opened rose. Write letters to distant friends. Savour each day. Write lists, if necessary, to set priorities. Do not fall into the 'terminal illness mentality' that robs people of quality time – when all thoughts are centred on the disease and not on the fun parts of life.

Rules change

One warm summer day, I visited a patient in his home. As I stood next to his bed, I looked up and could see into the garden where the sunlight was reflecting off a gleaming swimming pool. Surrounding the pool were spectacular rose bushes of every shade and colour, yet here lay this man in bed in a darkened room.

I looked at his wife and had a sudden inspiration. 'Is it possible for you to help Frank into a wheelchair?'

'Oh, certainly,' she answered. 'He can get in and out almost by himself as long as I stand close by to steady him.'

'How about taking him out to sit by the pool on nice days?' I enquired.

Both Frank and his wife looked at me as if I had just arrived from outer space. 'But Frank is very ill,' his wife said.

I took a deep breath and looked Frank in the eyes. 'Wouldn't you like to sit outside?' I asked, not worrying about trying to be tactful.

The couple exchanged looks and broke into smiles. 'I guess I never thought about it,' they admitted simultaneously.

It is common for people to do nothing but wait to get well from the common cold or flu. All past illnesses in our lives have been that way. With a terminal diagnosis, the rules of the game change. It is no longer a time of simply waiting; it is a time to take immediate action. What difference does it make if a terminally ill person sits by the pool instead of in bed? What difference does it make if he or she is exhausted after going out for dinner to their favourite restaurant? What difference do any of the silly little everyday things we usually worry about make now, when life is so precious?

Your choice

Do *whatever* you are able to do, *whenever* you are able. Let your body be your guide. Check with your medical team when in doubt, but use common sense and enjoy each moment. I do not suggest you take foolish risks, skip medication that is being given for comfort measures or defy your doctor's orders. The point is to think about your choices and how you can enjoy each and every day to the fullest.

Hospice patients are generally bed-bound or housebound, but not always. We once had a feisty lady in her seventies who had been in hospice for several months when she took a turn for the better. She decided to get out of bed, take herself out of hospice care and, to everyone's chagrin, she went on a cruise.

'I plan to *live* until I die,' she told the hospice staff as she packed her bags and departed. She took legal papers with her that would be handed to the captain of the ship in case she died at sea. She filled her suitcase with medication for emergencies. However, she did not die. She had a lovely time, gained six pounds and came home with a glowing suntan. She had often been extremely tired on the cruise, and had been forced to spend several days in bed, yet for the most part, the trip was fabulous. When she returned home, she showed visitors the slides of her trip and laughed heartily when she described her shipboard near-romance.

Another family packed up their van with an oxygen tank, medical supplies and one change of clothing and took off on a weekend retreat in the woods. They sang around the campfire and breathed the pine-scented air in carefree abandon, making memories to share for years to come.

People who are not physically strong enough to leave the house or travel can spend time writing letters to loved ones and having special quiet visits with friends and family. One man sat the video camera on a tripod and made a farewell video for his family with a loving message to each member. Let this be a time of personal choice, in which every moment is lived as fully as possible.

Relationships

An important part of everyday life is relating to those around you. You may have the gift of free time now you never had in the past. If you have a computer, begin to correspond by e-mail with long-lost acquaintances. Ask for a cordless phone next to your bed to allow the freedom to make calls when you feel up to it. And don't forget to include the younger generation in your schedule.

Children

It helps children to be involved in the care of a critically ill person, and it does not harm them. When I was 11 years old, I watched my grandmother in her final illness. My mother cared for her in our own home. It showed me, by example, what compassion is all about. I did not find it frightening; rather, the entire process felt completely natural. My family openly discussed what was happening and what we could expect in the future.

Do not hide illness and death from children. Allowing children to be a part of the process gives them a solid base from which to face major events in the future. When you protect your youngsters from life's imperfections, you don't give them a foundation to handle their own problems.

Be open with children

Even very young children are aware of major changes in a household. To suppose you are hiding anything from them is to deceive yourself. Be up-front and open with children. Explain the details of the disease as honestly as you can in age-appropriate terms. Children like to know what to expect and deserve to be included. Arm your family with books written for children about illness and death, and with materials that will help you explain illness and death to the children.

Be sure to explain the facts of your particular illness and to reassure children they will not get sick, too. Children are particularly egocentric and think of everything in terms of themselves. They may wonder if they caused your illness or if they are making you sicker because they are noisy or disobedient. Be sure they understand they are not responsible for your disease and make yourself available to answer any questions they might have.

Fear of abandonment

The fear of abandonment is common in children. Reassure your children they will be taken care of regardless of what happens to you, and include them in discussions of future plans. Fear and anger are closely related, so when young children do not understand the changes in their family or in the household, they may be afraid and act out of anger. They might get angry with you. Do not make them feel guilty about their emotions. By talking to children honestly and openly, you will help them overcome their fears and dissipate their anger.

Discipline

Even when there are changes in the household, it is important to continue to discipline children in the usual way. Rules give children a sense of security. The upheaval of the household can make them feel insecure, and a breakdown of rules only compounds their anxiety. Bedtimes need to remain constant, and so do rules about watching television or checking in with adults before going away from home.

When children act up, let them know you understand they are having a difficult time. Be sure to leave channels of communication open. Encourage them to ask questions and express themselves as much as they can. Usually children understand more than adults realize and it is helpful for the adults to know this.

Teenagers

Often teenagers react to difficulty by putting on a false mask of indifference. It may be because teens dislike being different from their peers. To have a terminally ill loved one does not fit into a teenager's scheme of being 'like everyone else'. They may feign nonchalance or act irritated over the inconvenience caused by the ill family member. Try not to take their indifference personally, or make the teenager feel guilty for not being more compassionate. The combination of the already over-stressed emotional upheavals of puberty and the disruption in a family with a life-threatening illness is a heavy load for a teenager to carry. Act accordingly and do not be offended by inappropriate teen behaviour. Acting 'cool' is a high priority for teens; do not mistake it for a lack of concern or love.

Extra support

Younger children and teenagers need to know they are still loved and important even if they have had to take a back seat when the normal routine is disturbed. Don't overload them with responsibilities if possible. Have someone in the household or a close family member available to encourage children and teenagers and oversee their care. Children need an adult to attend birthdays, graduations, sporting events and school activities. Ask other family members to attend special events in the children's lives when you cannot. Line up a caring relative or friend to stand in for you and your carers.

Other family members

Family members who do not live under the same roof as the person who is sick can sometimes be difficult. They do not share in your everyday progress and daily concerns. They may arrive on a bad day glowing with good health and full of humorous stories that are entirely inappropriate. This type of behaviour can cause hard feelings among you, the carer and your unintentionally blasé relative. Be as tolerant as possible and let other family member be your buffer zone if you are not able to deal with certain people or situations. Remind yourself that each moment is now precious and you do not have time for nursing hurts or resentful feelings.

Conserve your energy

It's not uncommon for relatives to pay inappropriately long visits, which may exhaust you. Your primary carer will become finely tuned to your needs and can help in this situation. Ask your carer to intercede and cut visits short, or to screen visitors when your energy level is low.

When my dad was ill, I listened with one ear when he had visitors. When I heard him becoming tired, I went into the room to fluff a pillow or offer a sip of water and asked Dad, 'Are you getting tired?' The visitors usually took their cue before Dad even responded and would get up to leave. It felt a bit sneaky, but it worked!

Family members can screen phone calls also. When energy is at a premium, conserve it for priority items. Ask others to do the jobs you cannot handle emotionally or physically.

Friends

Friends can be one of life's biggest blessings. When we are ill, they are the bright sunshine following a bleak thunderstorm. Let friends know if you are lonely *and* let them know when you are not feeling up to company. People are often uncomfortable with illness and steer clear of hospitals or sickrooms. You have to let them know you need them. Tell your friends they are not intruding, but are welcome, bright spots in your day. Invite a friend for a cup of tea if it has been a while since she has visited.

Let friends know when you need help. They may be eager to help and only waiting to hear from you. If you are at home, friends can take a big strain off your carer by allowing him or her to take a much-needed afternoon nap or leave the house to run errands. And they can help in other ways, too.

Clear the air

When visiting with friends, let them know you are aware of the seriousness of your illness and that they do not need to be embarrassed to talk about it. Clearing the air from the start allows for more honest visits in the future. One especially interesting patient I visited would announce her current medical condition on my arrival. She would recite it like a news bulletin, which ended with, 'End of medical report. Now let's talk about something interesting!' It was a comical way of setting the stage while letting me know what the status was. She never ceased to amuse me and I noticed she never lacked for visitors.

Losing friends

Unfortunately, certain friends disappear when illness arrives. This is common and natural. Try not to dwell on these broken relationships. New, unexpected friendships bloom in their place. Special people can come to comfort you as long as you keep the doors to your heart unlocked. Accept those who are willing to support and love you and who are able to face life-threatening illness. Forgive those who cannot.

Visitors

Any visitor, friend or relative can be a godsend at times and a problem at others. Concentrate on open communication with family members, and let others know your current needs. If you are ready to take a nap when someone shows up to visit, you may have to tell him or her you are not up to visiting. 'Would just a quick hug do for today?' you can ask.

Visitors respect your wishes and are thankful for your honesty. Nobody wants to cause undue strain. Often visitors only want to let you know they care. The amount of time they spend with you is secondary.

If you are uncomfortable with telling people you are not up to visiting, put the blame on somebody else. 'My wife says I'm only allowed visitors for 15 minutes because it wears me out too much', or some such remark should do the trick.

It's not rude or selfish to put your needs first when you are dealing with an illness that is sapping your strength. If you wish to have visitors be a blessing instead of a burden, express your wishes openly whether you are in the hospital or at home.

Communication

Different people serve different needs in your life. How you communicate with them varies. Regardless of the relationship, honesty is vital. Nobody can help ease your mind or be a true friend if you are putting up a false front. Do not say you are 'just fine' when you are not. Find ways to express yourself in a way that works best for you – whether through humour or writing.

Talk about plans

It is necessary to have an open discussion about your wishes in the event that you do not get well. Unfortunately, you may have to take the initiative for this conversation. There are many gentle ways to ease into this delicate subject matter. Remember to advance slowly.

Statements that begin with the word *if*, as in '*If* I don't get well, maybe we should talk about our options.' Or use the phrase *in case*. 'Let's get all our financial affairs in order *in case* I don't win the battle with this illness.' Families comfortable with using humour might introduce the subject of a terminal illness with dry humour: 'Don't start counting your inheritance yet, but the doctor doesn't seem to think I'm going to get well. Let's toss this idea around a bit.'

Make requests

In addition to 'if' and 'in case' statements, make 'I' statements. 'I really prefer to feed myself.' 'I'm not up to company right now.' Use statements that let others know exactly how you feel and what you need. Don't rely on wishy-washy questions like, 'Do you think I could feed myself?' or 'Should we invite Tom over?' Nobody can read your mind – you need to express your feelings. 'I' statements are straightforward and require less energy from everyone to interpret.

Health updates

Visitors may ask about your health, thinking you must want to talk about this subject. You don't need to spend too much time on medical details. Give a brief medical update and then tell your visitor you want to hear about his or her news, similar to the way my special patient did with her 'health updates' when she received visitors. It gives both of you a boost. Ask friends to bring photographs so you can share events that are important in their lives. You'll feel more a part of the world and you'll enjoy a refreshing break from the health-related issues that may otherwise preoccupy you.

Encourage your carer

Encourage your carer to maintain outside contacts. While I was caring for my father, I had a friend who would call almost every evening. He would ask about my dad and then about *my* day. There were times I would tell him I did not want to talk about my day. 'How about if you tell me a funny story instead?' I would ask, when I really needed a laugh. His stories took me out of my world of sickness for a little while and gave my spirits a genuine lift.

This same friend taught me not to accept 'OK' and 'just fine' as answers. 'Yeah, yeah,' he'd say to me when I said I was OK. Then he'd counter with, 'But, how are you *really*?' It taught me to be more honest expressing myself and to listen more carefully to others.

My three daughters also kept in touch with long-distance telephone calls, as did my husband. Every morning my Dad would ask if I had talked to my family the night before. If I answered, 'No', he would frown. 'You must talk to them every day,' he would insist, realizing the importance of those times of respite. I assured him I would call home more often and teased him about how high his phone bills were going to be.

Give your carers a break

Watch for signs of weariness in your carers. Suggest they invite a friend over or leave the house, if you can be left alone. Do not let everyone become consumed by your illness. Suggest playing a board game or renting a video. You may have more time to come up with ideas than the people who are involved in doing the everyday chores!

Express and share

Communication is far more than expressing needs and feelings. Your words can give someone a lift or express appreciation. Communication is also more than simply exchanging words. It is hearing an emotion, such as fear, in a person's voice, tuning into it and trying to help. It's someone saying, 'How are you *really*? Tell me about it.' Communication can be squeezing a hand when no words seem appropriate, or the acknowledgement of sad news with tear-filled eyes. Hugs and hearty laughter can also express your support.

Good communication is a top priority following a terminal diagnosis. Daily routines and relationships change. Now is the time to discuss all kinds of issues with the people around you and set priorities so you won't waste valuable time.

Priorities and goals

There is no better way to feel you still have some control over the course of your life than to set priorities or goals. They may be short-term goals and they may be different from those you had before your illness, but with them you can still be the one to make the decisions.

List your priorities on paper, and be as realistic as possible. An around-the-world cruise may not be possible but a trip to the beach with the family may be. Make reasonable plans and look forward to them. Have something on your calendar other than doctor's appointments.

Share your list with your loved ones, especially your primary carer, so you can work toward these goals together. Let people know you want to do as much for yourself as possible. Take over any chores you can handle physically. Maybe it was not your job previously to check the bank statement, but now you can manage that task easily and hand over cutting the lawn to your spouse. Make whatever changes seem necessary so your life has meaning and purpose each day. Let others know your priorities so they can help you achieve them.

Goals are important to your feeling of well-being. Short-term goals can be just as rewarding as long-term ones. Set simple daily objectives and some short-term goals for the month ahead. Make the goals reasonable. For example, plan to make a few phone calls to keep in contact with out-of-touch friends, or finish something tangible, such as a piece of needlework. Write down your plans and check them off when you complete each task. You'll feel a wonderful sense of accomplishment!

Live each day with as much quality as possible. The will to live is very strong. Take advantage of it! A strong self-will keeps hope alive.

A positive attitude and good thoughts can only help. Picture yourself as strong and healthy, and try to put a smile on your face whenever possible.

Positive thinking

Do not claim the illness as your own with statements such as, '*my* lung cancer' or '*my* liver ailment'. Do not show any acceptance toward this invasion against your good health. Remind yourself that the words you speak, aloud or in self-talk, can become fact. Be realistic, and positive rather than negative. Think of the illness as an enemy and actively fight it as you would any powerful foe.

Do not use mental imagery exclusively, ignoring your doctor's instructions, but do use it in connection with prayer and positive thinking. Acknowledge all aspects of your mental, physical and emotional healing. It may allow you to decrease your pain medication dosages and give you a sense of having some control over your body's condition.

I have been blessed with a wise husband who often straightens out my panicky thinking with a simple statement. We were six years into a local drought and it made everyone wary about future water rationing. I talked to my friends about it, frequently wondering what would happen to us. Should I plant flowers or not? I asked my daughters their opinions. Nobody had any answers. My husband was the only one to suggest I call our local water company and ask *them* what I should do.

I did just that. They told me how they were working to prevent rationing during the summer months. They could make no guarantees, but at least I had the latest, most correct information. I had restored my inner peace. When I relayed the information to my husband, he smiled smugly and said, 'It helps to go directly to the right source.'

Prayer

Prayer comforts many. When you are troubled or in doubt or need more information, you may want to ask God for answers, comfort and guidance as you face the days ahead.

Loneliness and isolation

You may feel overwhelmed by loneliness after your terminal diagnosis. You may feel nobody understands what you are going through. You may feel isolated by your inability to participate fully in activities.

Friends may be scared away by the notion of illness. If they don't know what to say or do, they may stop coming around. The feeling of abandonment is certainly real. You may have to reach out to others and make the first move. If you are having difficulty, seek professional help. Pastors, hospitals and doctors can refer you to a therapist or support group. If you are associated with a hospice organization, take advantage of their offer of a volunteer.

Get to know a volunteer

I was a volunteer coordinator for hospice for many years, and I can vouch for the caring individuals who go into that line of work. Hospice volunteers can be a great source of encouragement and strength to you and your family, filling the empty places in your lives and your hearts left by friends who are unable to cope.

Hospice volunteers are familiar with the subject of illness and death, and can offer you a vast array of knowledge from their personal experiences. They are generally available for a few hours each week for respite care, emotional support and any number of practical tasks. Don't miss this opportunity to make a new friend.

Get involved

If you feel isolated, put your imagination to work and find ways to become more involved with your family and the people around you. Whether you are at home or in a hospital, *speak up* when you need help. They can't know how you feel unless you tell them. If you miss your family because you don't share mealtimes with them, for example, ask them to join you for dessert – even if you are unable to eat a full meal.

Personalize your space

If you are in hospital or a hospice, ask to have personal articles like pictures or ornaments placed around you for a more homely atmosphere. Check with the staff for ways to feel less isolated; enquire about taking walks in the grounds using a wheelchair or taking your meals with others. If you are in a room by yourself, find out if another patient is also lonely and would appreciate a short visit from you.

Try something different

For the housebound, I have already suggested the bed be moved to a central location, rather than remain in a bedroom where it's easy to feel more isolated from daily activities. If you are uncomfortable with any set-up after trying it, gently ask that it be changed. Ask to come along for the ride in the car when errands are being run; a change of scene can do wonders for one's disposition! If you are bed-bound, invite people to sit on your bed. Loved ones may isolate you out of concern for your well-being, and not realize you feel left out. Tell them!

When my aunt became ill and was bed-bound, she would bang on her bed when she heard us laughing in the kitchen. 'Come and laugh in here with me!' she would urge us, and we all moved into her room and shared the joke. Unfortunately, there was no place close to the kitchen for her bed, but at least she let us know her needs.

Reach out

In this modern, electronic age we have new advances for beating loneliness. Cordless phones and personal computers can be purchased or borrowed and placed next to the bed. Ask for a telephone book and your personal address book to be placed nearby within easy reach. Receiving phone calls and using the telephone or computer can give you freedom.

Wheelchairs

Wheelchairs are also wonderful guards against loneliness. If you are unable to walk, you can use a wheelchair to move around the house and be with everyone else. Wheelchairs can also make outings easier and less tiring for you and your carers. Lightweight models fold easily for packing in cars.

A wheelchair can make the difference between sitting in a chair at home and being able to go for a walk in the mall or for a stroll in the park. Anywhere you go you find people in wheelchairs; it is no longer unusual. Restaurants accommodate people in wheelchairs; so do shopping centres and public toilets. This kind of building design is called 'disabled access'. If you expect to go out often, apply for a 'disabled' sticker for your car from social services so that you can park in designated areas and enjoy easy access to buildings.

Role changes and values

Household roles change with illness. Your partner may now do the kitchen chores while you plan the meals. The delicate balance and role changes can make the household feel unsettled. Not everyone is comfortable in new roles that previously 'belonged' to another member of the household. Talk about these feelings and try to divide and delegate tasks in the most practical way possible.

Fortunately, roles are not as carefully defined today as they were 20 years ago, so these changes are not as disruptive to the young people or the adults performing them. Men do the laundry, cook meals and hoover the carpets as well as women.

The daily routine

Keep the daily routine as normal as possible, even if the household roles change. When a household runs smoothly, it is easier for family members to deal with necessary disruptions. Frequently it is the small inconveniences that disturb a peaceful environment and raise the stress level. Keeping the laundry up to date so that nobody runs out of socks, having milk in the fridge so that nobody has to skip their morning cereal, paying the bills so that the phone does not get cut off are all necessary tasks that make the bigger problems easier to face.

If you have to delegate chores from bed, do so. Make lists of what needs to be done, then check them off as you find volunteers to do the jobs. Take up those offers of 'let me know if I can do anything to help' that frequently come from friends and family. Be sure to save practical tasks for your hospice volunteer if you have one.

Let children be children

When it is necessary to change roles, children often enjoy the variety. However, remember that children need to remain children. I have heard adults tell a young boy that because his father was ill, the boy was now 'the man of the house'. Do not place enormous demands like this on childen. Assure children that the adults of the family will continue to take care of them. You can ask children to do extra chores, within reason. But be careful not to make them feel like they have to become adults overnight and shoulder the whole load.

Children can help

Children make good helpers and are usually willing to run upstairs for a blanket or go to the kitchen for a glass of water. They have more energy, and their legs can be put to good use as long as they are not overburdened or have to neglect their own activities.

Chores may change from day to day and the household situation may be re-evaluated many times so it can run most efficiently with the least effort. Be sure your children know you appreciate their extra help and that the situation is temporary.

Children love it when adults stop their frantic activities, give them attention and make eye contact. Do not feel bad that you cannot go outside and toss a ball to your son, for example. He will probably be just as content to have you help him build a model aeroplane or simply read the instructions to him while he does the work. It is educational for children to be a part of a household that is caring for someone with a catastrophic illness.

Make it fun for children to help

My babies were all Caesarean births. When I came home from the hospital with my third child, my two toddlers were a great help. I asked them to 'Please pat the baby until I can get in there', or had them reach into a bottom drawer for me, which saved me much painful movement. I was careful to make the chores fun.

When I needed to rest, we all climbed on to my big bed and looked at picture-books while I rested. I knew they were safe and couldn't get into anything as long as they remained on the bed with me. They loved the extra attention, even though my eyes were shut, as long as I remembered to respond to their questions with an occasional 'Uh-huh'.

They were excited to help with the new baby and we all worked together as a family. Even so, I was quick to reassure them that, 'Next week Mummy won't need as much help.' In the evening, when Daddy was home, the kids got to be kids again and not just Mummy's helpers.

Children, even young children, learn more from watching than from lectures. When children see a family working together and caring for a family member who is ill, they learn about compassion and love. It shows them that families stick together through tough times and that love flows even more freely during desperate hours.

Decisions

Among the decisions people with terminal illness must make is one concerning the disposal of material goods.

Giving away personal belongings

My mother began giving away personal belongings years before she died. At first it bothered me terribly. 'Why are you doing this?' I asked. 'You're in perfect health.' I did not want to face the fact that a day would come when my mother would no longer be around. But after years of watching her give away her belongings, I came to understand and appreciate her philosophy.

At first she laughed and made light of it, shrugging it off by saying it would make less for her to dust. But as she got older, and the family became accustomed to her dividing up her precious items, we came to see she took great pleasure in this task. When I got married more than 30 years ago, she packed boxes of things for me to take, telling me the story behind each of the items. 'This is the tablecloth that was purchased for my bridal shower,' she said as she packed a large, white lace tablecloth. 'This is Spode china,' she told me as she packed the next item. It gave her great joy to share with her loved ones instead of waiting for us to inherit her things when she could not see our appreciation or enjoy the pleasure of giving them away.

When her granddaughters got married, she repeated the process. She got out boxes and filled them. Every time I visited her, she would ask, 'What do you want to take home with you?' Eventually, it no longer embarrassed me. I understood completely. There was an itemized list in her dresser drawer of things she insisted certain people have. The list made her feel secure.

How to part with belongings

Part of saying goodbye is parting with material objects. If you feel uncomfortable about giving material items to friends and family, at least make a list stating anything in particular you want someone to have. Is there an item several people will want? Designate who is to have it. I have helped some of my hospice patients label the backs or undersides of items with a person's name so there is no question about who is to have it.

This preparation is not morbid. It allows you to have some control over the disposition of your worldly goods. When you are no longer around, these material items may console loved ones. All over my house, I have small mementoes of loved ones who have died, just as I have gifts from loved ones who are still living. I think about these people as I dust the item or water the plants they have given me, and it makes me feel closer to them. Of course I would remember them without the material item, but it is comforting to touch something they once owned and touched and cared enough to leave with me.

Choose the method that feels most natural. Leave a detailed list, mark items well or present the gift yourself. People may react differently if you give them a special item; some will be pleased and some may be unable to handle it. Accept that there are no right or wrong feelings and it may take time for them to appreciate the gift. Often, giving away belongings opens the door to meaningful dialogues about life and death, and has a cleansing effect for everyone. Hospice volunteers can be a big help with this task. Ask for their advice and let them help you label or bestow items.

Legal matters

In addition to personal closure, saying goodbye and distributing material goods, having everything in legal order improves your peace of mind. Legal issues vary, but the important aspects are universal. The following section guides you through what to consider at this time.

A will

Everyone needs a will. People are always telling me they do not need a will because they do not have anything to bequeath. I repeat, *everyone* needs a will, regardless of your situation. It must be current and it must be in writing.

Ask for help at your local Citizens Advice Bureau about appropriate forms. You do not need to see a solicitor if you have a simple estate. Just follow the instructions on the forms carefully; they are uncomplicated and thorough.

For other options, consult your solicitor. If you are a pensioner you may be eligible for free legal advice. Making a will need not be an ordeal or a financial burden. Be sure your will is signed according to the instructions and notarized, if necessary. Put it in a safe place and let family members know where it is. Have several copies, perhaps one in a safety deposit box, one with a trusted family member, one with a solicitor and a copy for each person who is mentioned in the will.

If children are involved, be sure the people you have chosen as guardians have agreed to rear your children and that the financial arrangements involved are spelled out.

Living wills or advance directives

Another legal document that should be in order is an advance directive (or living will). These are instructions for life-sustaining equipment and resuscitation orders when you are unable to let others know your wishes. It is very important to have the legal documents for this on file. Also make sure your family members are aware of your wishes.

Do you need a living trust? Do you wish your property to go

immediately to your heirs? Should you make immediate provisions to take advantage of tax breaks? Have you appointed an executor? If a large estate is involved, it is imperative to make an appointment with an accountant or a lawyer.

Power of attorney

It is also helpful to have a trusted second party who is able to sign cheques on your accounts. This is called giving someone the power of attorney. A time may come when someone else must pay your bills and withdraw cash from your account. This is much easier to do if a second party is prepared and authorized to do this *before* the need becomes urgent. Bills arrive regardless of what is going on in a household.

When my mother had a heart attack and was hospitalized suddenly, a power of attorney made life much simpler. My sister could keep up with the post and pay the bills. Conversely, when my neighbour was hospitalized suddenly, nobody could sign his cheques or had a key to his house. By the time he was released from hospital, his utilities had been disconnected, and all sorts of messes had to be straightened out at unnecessary expense and great inconvenience.

Legal documents

It is never too soon to take care of legal matters, and it is simple to keep them updated. Getting everything in order will give you peace of mind and is a gift you give your loved ones to save them undue problems and stress in the future.

Make a special, well-marked folder of important documents to make it easier for others to handle any legal issues. Keep the following documents in the folder:

- durable power of attorney
- resuscitation orders
- life insurance policies
- National Insurance certificate
- driver's licence
- birth certificate
- marriage certificate
- bank books
- military discharge papers
- stock certificates or records
- property holdings
- organ donor card

- phone numbers of doctors, funeral directors, and anyone else who needs to be contacted about your condition

About suicide

I read somewhere that suicide hotlines receive a vast number of telephone calls from people with terminal illnesses. I decided to check into this and called three suicide hotlines to ask for statistics. I was told none were available. The people I spoke with claimed they had very few calls from terminal patients themselves. However, they did get many phone calls from the carers of terminally ill patients who were concerned that their loved ones might be suicidal.

Statistics show that when people are without hope they consider suicide. I have tried to stress in this book that even when there is nothing more that can be done medically, there *is* still hope. When a doctor says nothing more can be done, it means no further medical treatment or medication can improve the condition. The symptoms caused by the illness can still be treated to bring about comfort, if not a cure. The body may restore itself to good health or remain uncured without getting any worse for years. Remember: miracles do happen. There is always hope.

Feeling worthy

People often equate productivity with worthiness. The idea is, the more you do, the better you feel about yourself. When illness hits and you have to take time to allow your body to mend, stopping your regular activities may devastate you. You are still worthy, even when you are 'nonproductive' in the usual sense of the word. You are still who you are, even when you are ill. Your loved ones love you because of who you are, not what you do. Whether you are winning a marathon race or merely holding a hand while sick in bed does not change who you are. Concentrate on the meaningful things that remain in your life, such as providing love, encouragement, laughter and prayers, instead of what is no longer possible.

I love you just the way you are

Christopher Reeve, the actor best known for his role as Superman, was paralysed from the neck down in an equestrian accident in 1995. In 1998, he wrote his story in his autobiography, *Still Me*.

Immediately following his accident he was unable to speak because of the respirator. He mouthed the words, 'Maybe we should let me go,' to his wife, Dana. She started to cry and said, 'I am only going to say this once: I will support whatever you want to do, because this is your life and your decision. But I want you to know that I'll be with you for the long haul, no matter what.' Then Reeve writes, 'She added the words that saved my life: "You're still you. And I love you." '

According to Reeve, his family continually reassures him that they love him for who he is, not for the roles he played in the past, his financial successes, his athletic prowess or his fame.

If suicidal thoughts creep in, share them with someone who can help you sort them out. Suicide is a tragic end to life. Be aware it leaves wounds, often untreatable ones, in those left behind.

I know of two terminally ill patients who committed suicide. The aftermath was heartbreaking. The loved ones they left behind experienced waves of guilt for many years. They blamed themselves for not seeing it coming and preventing the suicidal act. The suddenness of the death denied them the pleasure of taking care of their loved ones. They were denied any feeling of closure, making the period of grief much more intense, difficult and lengthy. One woman was left financially strapped due to a suicide clause in her husband's life insurance policy of which he was probably unaware.

The two men who committed suicide were likely thinking they would save everyone a lot of trouble if they removed themselves before they became a burden to others. But instead of their deaths making life easier, they left a path of wreckage behind, wreckage that can never be undone – words left unsaid, and guilt that nags for ever.

Get help

If you feel beyond hope and think you are a burden to your loved ones or are draining financial resources, discuss the situation with someone – a friend, relative or professional. Allow them to help you sort out the truth from your desperate feelings.

3
Spiritual approaches

Before your illness did you feel like you were in charge of your life? Did you make long-range plans expecting them to work out? Did you set goals, confident that you would reach them? With the onset of a critical illness, you were probably rudely reminded that life was not in your control after all.

Give up control

Prior to your illness, you might have had only tiny indications that your fate was not in your control. When a flat battery kept you from attending an appointment or bad weather caused you to cancel a long-awaited picnic, your sense of security was temporarily disturbed. In the past, you could remedy these problems by calling a mechanic or postponing the picnic until the next day. Then you smiled, raring to go, and thought you had matters under control again. These little changes in plans merely stopped you momentarily, but they did not convince you that you were not the one in charge.

Critical illness interrupts your careful plans. Reality grabs you and shakes you, making your sense of security fall to the ground in a heap. You will have to give in to a stronger force and admit life is now out of your hands – one of the most difficult tasks of dealing with a terminal diagnosis.

Let go of struggle

As soon as people, sick or well, let go of control, life becomes less a struggle and more a pleasant journey. Have you ever had a sock-pull with a puppy? The harder you try to pull the sock away, the tighter the puppy hangs on. As soon as you let go of your end, he usually drops his end, too, perks up his ears, wags his tail and waits for the battle to begin again.

An incurable illness can also become a power struggle. The harder you try to hang on emotionally the less strength you have to combat the illness physically. Use your strength wisely. Instead of tugging for control, like the puppy, let go of your end. If you are unaccustomed to giving up control it may be difficult at first. You will naturally want to fight back. However, continue letting go, even when you feel it isn't working.

Prayer and soul-searching

Now is a great time for deep soul-searching. Before you were ill you may have been too busy to have time for soul-searching. Take time to think about what you believe in. Develop your faith and beliefs so they can support you in the days ahead.

For many prayer is a powerful form of practising their faith. Prayers do not have to be fancy or structured. Prayer can be a great source of comfort and can give you inner strength in quiet, dark moments. Talk to God as you would a good friend. Tell God your fears and your hopes. Allow this to be a special time of spiritual communion.

As you practise, your faith will increase and eventually come from your heart instead of your head. When you release your heavy burden, you will be filled with inner peace. The torrential winds that tossed you around will calm down and you will be able to stand firm and strong. I have a friend who says, 'You can't direct the winds, but you can certainly adjust your sails!' Adjusting your sails allows you to be tranquil rather than engage in a torrential struggle.

Praying can also take place in the form of listening. If we do all the talking, we can miss important messages. Try to spend some wordless, quiet time in thought. Inner healing often takes place during times of quiet solitude.

Trying to understand illness

Illness is beyond the realm of human understanding. Who can comprehend the purpose for a young husband, eagerly awaiting the birth of his first child, being diagnosed with a malignant brain tumour? Or the reason a teenager contracts the AIDS virus from a blood transfusion? Who can explain why chemotherapy works on one patient and not another? Why can't the medical profession have more definite answers about cures or a prognosis?

No easy answers

Struggling to find answers to unanswerable questions only wastes precious time and energy. Instead, search for ways to obtain inner peace. When tragedy hits, people can be overwhelmed and their faith can falter. They are often angry, desperate and filled with fear. But worst of all, nobody seems to understand. If you feel this way, look for a friend or a pastor who does understand. Or join a support group.

Expressing your feelings to others helps relieve the emotional pain. Hospitals offer these kinds of groups. Find one that works for you.

Faith and trust

Life may seem senseless, but with time its purpose will unfold. God has plans that do not always match our own. It can be difficult fitting the pieces of the puzzle together when you do not know what the completed picture is supposed to look like! This is where faith and trust take over.

Make amends

In addition to giving up the desire to control your future, let go of problems from the past. Hanging on to them can disturb the peaceful quality you want in your life. Broken relationships and hostile feelings only stand in the way of enjoying whatever time remains.

When each moment is valuable, do you want a closet filled with bitterness, anger, hate, grudges, fear and rage? Or do you want to fill that space with love, joy, peace, serenity and tranquillity? The decision is yours. Others do not 'make' you feel angry or guilty or bitter. They may do things that cause you to feel a certain way, but they are not responsible for your feelings. Each person owns his own feelings. Do you have feelings you do not like? Hurtful ones? Destructive ones? Are you allowing them to live within you as a parasite, draining your well-being and serenity?

Work out negative feelings

Negative feelings hurt the people who possess them, not the recipient. Negative feelings or grudges prevent good feelings from surfacing. Only if you remove negative feelings can you replace them with peace, joy, happiness and tranquillity.

I have a friend who knows who he is and what he stands for. He refuses to return hostility with hostility. He does not let others decide how he should feel. Praise does not give him a feeling of false euphoria, nor does criticism tear him down. Snubs do not hurt him and he does not become depressed when others treat him unfairly.

'To let another person determine whether I am rude or gracious, elated or depressed, is to relinquish control over my own personality.'

If you have been treated unfairly or hurt by others in the past, think about this concept. You may agree that what others have thought about you in the past really doesn't matter when your sense of self-worth comes from within.

Part of the forgiveness process is to make amends and get rid of ill feelings towards other people. This step can reinforce your feelings of self-worth. Make a list, mentally or on paper, of relationships that need mending. Have you exchanged harsh words with certain people? Do you hold a grudge towards anyone who has treated you unfairly? Has money come between you and a friend? Think carefully as you make your list.

When the list is complete, think about ways to resolve your feelings. Reflection may help you forgive those on your list. Then meet with those involved, if you can, and clear the air. Do not expect others to change because you have contacted them. The point of contacting them is so you can offer forgiveness and friendship unconditionally. Even if your efforts are refused, it's all right. What's important for your well-being is to erase your own 'emotional chalkboard', forgive others, rid yourself of any negative feelings and start fresh.

If you cannot meet personally with someone on your list, make contact by letter or telephone. If direct contact is impossible (for example, the person has died), you can still write a letter of forgiveness. The act of writing is the important part; you don't have to post what you wrote. Forgiveness does not come from outside you; it comes from within your heart. You can experience a complete cleansing and feel more at peace by forgiving others, regardless of their response.

Make peace with God

In addition to making amends with earthly relationships, you may need to mend your relationship with God. Perhaps you never felt you needed this relationship or maybe you never had an opportunity to pursue it. There is a parable about workers in a field. It tells about some men who worked in a field from early morning and about others who showed up at various times during the day, with the last group arriving and working only an hour. When the workers were paid at the end of the day, they all received the same wages. The early arrivals complained, saying they should have been paid more, but God declared it was his desire to pay everyone the same wages. In his eyes, all receive the same rewards regardless of the time served.

It is not too late either to begin or to renew a personal relationship with God. Faith can be a great comfort as you approach the unknown.

When it comes to religion or faith, some people feel like hypocrites turning to religion only now, when they are desperate.

'I never had any time for that religious stuff when I was well,' one man told me. I explained that faith is like a come-as-you-are party. Everyone is invited and it involves no special clothing or requirements.

If you have any doubts about your spiritual life, call on your religious community and ask for a visit from a clergy member, priest or rabbi. They are usually more than happy to make a home visit and answer any questions you may have.

Receiving the Sacraments

For Christians, the sacraments of baptism and Holy Communion are available even during illness.

Baptism

You may wish to be baptized as an outward sign of your new or renewed faith. If you are still mobile, you may want to find a church where you feel comfortable and discuss baptism with the priest or pastor.

Being bed-bound or housebound does not mean you are unable to be baptized. Make some telephone calls or ask a trusted person to make them for you. Most hospitals have chaplains on call, or on their staff, who will be glad to visit you and make the necessary arrangements. Catholic priests are very comfortable with baptisms in private homes or hospitals. Churches that baptize by immersion have a bit of a logistics problem, but nothing is impossible.

Holy Communion

Holy Communion does not have to be performed exclusively in a church either. Most churches have volunteers who take out the sacraments to any of their homebound or hospitalized parishioners. Some have a special little case fitted to carry the elements and supplies. It gives great comfort to those who cannot get to church. Volunteers will usually visit anyone who is too ill to attend church, regardless of whether they are active church members, non-practising or newly converted.

I have been called upon in many situations to contact a clergy member, rabbi or priest to perform various rites or ceremonies. I have always been treated kindly and received prompt attention. You do not have to be in a church to pray or talk to God. It is not necessary to be in a church to be baptized or to take communion. The rituals and sacraments are available for the asking.

Find what works for you

Regardless of your religious beliefs or background, now may be the time to delve into spiritual support. Plug into this source of help and draw strength from it for both yourself and your family. All it takes to contact a religious community is a telephone call and an explanation of the situation to get caring people to visit. Don't be embarrassed to request favours from a religious community you aren't a member of – people are happy to help.

If, by chance, you do not get a positive and prompt response to your needs, contact another church or temple. Messages do get lost, telephone numbers do get copied down incorrectly, and calls do get postponed due to an emergency situation or crisis. Be persistent! The comfort you receive from your religious contacts is too important to neglect.

How to say goodbye

When you have completed the task of making amends and forgiving others, it may be time to contact other special people in your life. Make a list of anyone to whom you wish to give a special message. It's easy to get so caught up in doing the laundry and getting to work on time that we forget to tell people how much we love them and thank them for the part they have played in our lives.

Now that you have faced your mortality and are doing a thorough job of internal 'housekeeping', you will probably feel a need to complete any unfinished business. Making a list on paper helps you feel more organized and also lets you see how much you are accomplishing in emotional tasks.

Personal messages

Have you told your loved ones how much they mean to you? Have you told them the reasons you find them so special? Saying, 'I love you', is fine, but heartfelt, personal messages are more meaningful. Messages such as, 'The way you smile all the time has filled my life with happiness', or 'You've been such a good sport through the bad times, and I really appreciate that about you', are more special.

The remarks I remember most from my deceased loved ones are not the big declarations of love, but the sincere statements that came straight from their hearts. One such message came from my Aunt Bea just days before she died. It was difficult for her to speak and even more difficult for her to form coherent ideas. Her expression suggested she was going to say something profound. When she finally spoke she said, 'June, I've always thought you have such a nice face.'

Now, that may not sound like a great compliment, but many years later it still touches me so deeply that tears run down my face as I write about it. If Aunt Bea had told me I was beautiful or even pretty it would have been a far cry from the truth. I would have brushed off such statements as empty compliments.

But it has always been very important to me to have people feel comfortable around me. I do not want them to feel intimidated. I want people to like and trust me. To accomplish these goals, I need to look like a nice person; I need to have a 'nice face'. That message must have come straight from my aunt's soul. Profound? Poetic? No, but to tell me I have a nice face is the dearest thing anyone could say to me. I will treasure it for the rest of my life.

Goodbyes can be messages expressed with simple words. The messages do not have to be articulate or profound. They need only come from deep within your heart.

While my father was in his final illness, he told all of us how much he loved us. When he told my mother he loved her, he always added, 'And I'll love you even more after I'm gone.' I didn't realize at the time what a loving legacy he was leaving behind until a few weeks after his death. Mom told me she could still feel Dad's love. 'He loves me even more now that he's gone, you know,' she said often. Dad's oft-repeated phrase continued to surface and smoothed her transition into life without him.

My mother lived well into her eighties. After my father died, my mom and I became more aware of the fragility of life. We would always say goodbye with a simple 'I love you.' I would share a memory with her to let her know what a wonderful mother she had been. If she praised me, I would respond with, 'That's because you raised me right,' or some such remark. I remind myself to do likewise with my own children and grandchildren, expressing my love and special feelings toward them frequently, while I have the chance.

Understanding death

There are many aspects of life that human beings will never fully understand. Along with not understanding the reasons for some people being struck down by illness, we are also unable to understand completely the concept of death, or what happens after death. There are many perspectives on what happens after death. Explore your religious tradition's beliefs on the subject.

Final arrangements

Along with the tasks of making amends and getting legal affairs in order, comes the opportunity to make known your wishes about final arrangements. Some people even choose to make their own funeral arrangements. Tom was such a person.

After the doctor told him he had only a short time left, he drove to a funeral home and talked to the director. Then he went to two other funeral homes. He picked up price lists, went home and compared, and a few days later completed the arrangements, even paying for the services in advance.

'I don't want my family to have to do these things,' he told me. He also went to the cemetery, chose a plot, ordered a grave marker and paid for those. He did these tasks by himself and felt very good about them. As an engineer, he was an efficient, well-organized person and this was part of his nature. He had always sheltered his loved ones from unpleasantness and that was exactly what he was doing now. When he told me about it, he never shed a tear. He reported the facts and showed me the paperwork. As my eyes brimmed with tears, I asked if the work had been difficult for him.

'Yeah,' he finally admitted, 'it wasn't a lot of fun. But I'm glad I did it. It feels really good now.' Then he smiled and said smugly, 'And this way I'm sure it got done properly.'

Tom was a special person. He was only 50 years old and put up a real physical battle against his illness. He lived two years longer than anyone expected. During that time, he was a prolific list maker. In addition to the final arrangements, he planned his own funeral service. He spoke at length to his pastor and made it clear he wanted a celebration of life and not a drab, depressing service. He wanted lively music, including 'It's Only Just Begun' and 'Jesus Loves Me' sung by his grandchildren. He listed poems he wanted read and designed an order of service that included a black-and-white photograph of himself. On the back cover, with the photograph, was the message, 'See ya, pal', which was the way he always said goodbye.

Next he chose the clothing he wished to be buried in and purchased a special striped shirt. I had to laugh when his wife told me she had finally drawn the line when he wanted to choose her outfit, too. 'He's just too much,' she said with a grin and shook her head in disbelief.

Tom was definitely more thorough than most people, and I was concerned that these plans were occupying too much of his time, yet they seemed to bring him comfort. It appeared to be his way of completing his obligations on earth before preparing to depart. His family agreed that this was simply Tom's way. He had always been a meticulous person and threw himself into every task.

About a month before he died, Tom took a turn for the worse. He called his family together and invited his pastor over for a time of fellowship and communion. The newest little member of the family was baptized right on Tom's bed, and the adult members took communion together. They prayed and sang their favourite hymns while Tom's son strummed a guitar.

This may not be the way every family wants to deal with impending death, but it worked for Tom and his family. There are no rules to follow and no set procedures that need to be adhered to at this time of life. Each family and each person needs to do what he thinks is best. This is a family time, when the heart should be the guide and protocol can be set aside.

Although Tom made all the arrangements himself, his family had a set procedure for funerals and he kept within those boundaries, protecting the comfort zones of all involved. Tom checked the plans as he went along and they served his family well. He felt he saved them pain by doing it himself, and tying up loose ends gave him a feeling of accomplishment.

What's best for your family

Tom's plans were carried out successfully. Nevertheless, at times the loved one's plans do not work. One of my patients insisted funerals were barbaric. 'I want nothing when I go,' she told me and her family. 'No wake, no viewing, no service, no grave. Just have me cremated and scattered. I don't want my family to have any bother or expense.' We didn't argue with her.

Several months later when she died, I was called to the house. When I arrived, her son was on the telephone busily contacting funeral homes. He put together an elaborate traditional funeral complete with wreaths, a limousine, a two-day wake, a church service and a cemetery burial. There was music, a soloist and a big reception afterwards. I tried to hide my surprise. Then he explained, 'I'm doing this for my dad and my siblings. They need it and so do I. Mom would understand.' After attending the service I had to agree. It *was* necessary. In this situation it was necessary for the living, and his mom *would* have understood. Cost, location, the time element and personal feelings cannot always be best determined before an event.

Funeral rituals are for the living. They offer rites of passage, and they are an opportunity to gather people together who can offer support in the future. The hugs and love shared at a funeral nurture and sustain those who are left behind.

Decisions

Many decisions need to be made regarding final arrangements. It is especially difficult for your family to make these decisions if they have no idea about your preferences. Every situation and every person is unique. Not everyone is like Tom, who took care of each tiny detail himself. There is no right or wrong in this area; do what makes you and your family most comfortable.

Regardless of whether or not you personally take over the tasks, it is particularly important to let your wishes be known. You lift a great burden of indecision and anxiety from your loved ones' shoulders by doing so. You can make it easier for your family if you leave an addendum to your instructions with permission to make changes if they choose.

Expressing your choices

You can let your family know what kind of funeral you would like in various ways. Talk openly about your wishes if family members are comfortable doing it this way. If not, write down the details and give the list to a trusted friend, hospice volunteer or relative, to be referred to when the information is needed.

If you find that writing or talking about these delicate matters is too difficult, try putting the information on an audio- or videotape. I was once given an audiotape with a finely detailed message from a hospice patient to his family. His family appreciated it, and it made their job much easier knowing they were carrying out his intentions as closely as possible.

Pastors are generally comfortable discussing final arrangements, especially if they will be conducting the service. Patients with terminal illnesses often discuss with their pastors religious readings or poems they wish to be read and the music they want played or sung. They may designate a special friend to help the pastor in the eulogy. Some people wish to write a personal message to be read during the service.

The choices are endless. If you have no preferences, it is just as important to let that fact be known. My father left a single sheet of paper with instructions numbered in the order they were to be carried out, which made it very easy for us. But his most thoughtful gesture came in the postscript at the bottom of the page. He wrote, 'These are my preferences, but feel free to change anything.' We followed most of his instructions, but when something seemed impractical or illogical, we knew we had the freedom to choose otherwise and were not left feeling guilty afterward.

Choices

The following list of general items can help you become familiar with some of the options. For more details or explanations of the terms, see final arrangements, pages 103–10.

- Traditional service followed by burial
- Traditional service followed by cremation
- Memorial service only
- Graveside service only
- Speakers
- Music-specific soloists or musicians
- Scripture choices
- Fraternal organization involvement
- Pastor, minister, priest, rabbi or other person to conduct service
- Preference of religious denomination or church
- Clothing choice – formal versus informal
- Obituary – any particular information to be included
- Flowers or donations to a specific charity
- Any special reading or message to be included in the programme
- Military affiliation to be contacted, if any
- Photos to be displayed
- Out-of-town people who need to be notified

Financial arrangements

If you are a veteran or are entitled to special benefits through any insurance policies or organizations, let your loved ones know how to best obtain these funds. Insurance companies cannot settle a claim unless they are notified. Be sure none of your benefits are overlooked due to lack of information. Keep policies in an accessible place.

If there is a family burial plot, let your carer or loved ones know. Try not to leave loose ends that may cause frustrating snags or financial losses for your loved ones, such as unresolved credit disputes. If you intend to leave special instructions, make sure they are easy to find and follow. If you choose to participate actively in the plans, do only as much as you can comfortably handle each day. Plan your schedule around the times when you are most rested and ask for as much help and support as you need.

Gently remind yourself that your participation is a generous, loving gift you are giving your loved ones.

Live each moment

After the details have been settled, you can put aside the thoughts of final arrangements and concentrate on living each moment as it is. All of life is a process – a time of change and growth. I have seen relationships heal and reconciliation blossom for individuals after a life-threatening diagnosis.

When the days of doctors' appointments and trips for treatment are over, you can move on to other things. When the legal paperwork and financial affairs are all in order, you can relax. When you have taken care of final arrangements, written down your preferences or discussed your wishes with a trusted person, you can feel at peace. After you have mended any broken relationships, said your formal farewells and put your spiritual life in order, then what?

Then simply live each moment to its fullest! Some days will be more difficult than others. However, no matter what your physical capabilities, you can always pray, smile and dispense love and affection. Every physical accomplishment is mere icing on the cake. Each smile, each hug, each giggle is something to appreciate and savour.

Life is good indeed if you take pleasure in the little things that healthy people do not notice. Don't fight the situation, but instead look forward to the adventure ahead. Swim with the current instead of struggling upstream. Allow your loved ones to wrap you in a blanket of love that will keep you safe and warm as you prepare to leave them.

PART 2
The Carer

4

Your role as carer

It is one of the most beautiful compensations of this life that no man can sincerely try to help another without helping himself.

Ralph Waldo Emerson

One of the most difficult yet rewarding jobs a person can tackle is that of a primary carer. The primary carer is the person who promises to 'give care' to someone, whatever it may entail, for the duration of an illness.

A full-time primary carer or several carers doing shifts may be required for a terminally ill patient. And even when the patient is being treated in an acute-care hospital or admitted to a convalescent home, they will still need a carer to oversee their physical, emotional and spiritual care.

A friend or relative usually oversees the care, spends the majority of time at the bedside, and is considered the main carer. He or she is the most affected if the patient does not get well. In the following chapters, I address family members and friends who are carers for their loved ones who are in hospice, the hospital or at home.

Why be a carer?

When a person is terminally ill, it is not ordinarily possible to look ahead to a time when the person is cured and able to care for themselves. Instead, the future will probably hold days filled with the process of dying, followed by a period of bereavement over the loss of a loved one. Stated in stark black-and-white, that may look like a depressing, overwhelming task, but it isn't. For someone to allow you to share in his or her last moments is a rare gift to treasure.

The months, weeks and days following the end of medical treatment can be the most cherished time in a person's life. This can be a time of reconciliation, restoration, love and spiritual growth. To be a part of the dying process is as precious as being a part of the birth process. Both are brief yet significant moments that can enrich your own life tremendously. To avoid either experience is to miss an incredible opportunity to grow as a person.

Fulfilment

I worked in the hospice field for more than 12 years serving as a volunteer coordinator, hospice volunteer and grief support group leader. During that period, I also cared for my terminally ill father, mother, aunt and several friends. It was the most fulfilling period of my life. I felt as if each day really counted, and every night I went to sleep knowing I had accomplished something important.

The hospice volunteers I recruited and trained were the very salt of the earth. In addition to being my co-workers, many became my dearest friends. Our lives were rich and meaningful. We helped each other and shared experiences as we learned about the process of dying and the stages of bereavement.

We did our own grieving, too, when a patient or family member died. Yet, in spite of my own suffering, those years provided some of my fondest memories. Occasionally I still counsel a terminal patient or griever, even though I am officially retired. Those sessions oil the mechanisms of my heart and make it beat more happily.

The information discussed in this section comes from my personal experiences and those of other hospice volunteers. I know you will find your role as carer a positive, life-changing experience, too.

Be honest

When you decide to be the main carer for a loved one, let them know you are comfortable with your new role. Openly express your desire to stand by them through whatever the remaining time brings. Express any doubts you may have so you can work them out now instead of later, during a crisis. Talk about who you can ask for extra help. Discuss home care and hospital care, letting them know if you are willing to be in charge for the duration of the illness. Talk about insurance benefits and all the issues mentioned on page 67.

The job of carer is demanding and, in the beginning, may seem to be without reward. Rarely, if ever, is a carer asked, 'How are you doing?' yet almost every person who walks into the room asks the patient how he is. Carers are expected to have endless energy, Atlas-like strength and no life of their own. A carer needs to remember that this neglect or lack of appreciation is not due to thoughtlessness; it is due to ignorance. People who have not been carers may not understand or appreciate the role. Once you have been a carer, you will remember to give praise and assistance to others.

When AIDS was first discovered, much mystery surrounded the illness. It hit the gay community especially hard, and many AIDS patients were without family support. We now realize AIDS is not an exclusively gay disease and touches all groups. In the 1980s, there were no support groups, and funds for hospice care were not yet available. At the time, I read several articles about members of the gay community stepping in and filling the care-providing void. It was an impressive show of support. The carers set up schedules and rotated shifts so the patients always had care available.

When people live with the threat of a terminal illness, they are quick to take care of each other, not knowing if they may be the next one to need care. Those of us not living under such tenuous conditions can easily overlook that some day we may need care ourselves. We blithely take good health for granted and act as if life will go on forever.

As the gay community watched their peers die in great numbers during the 1980s, they no longer felt infallible or immortal. They practised love and human kindness as a result of the sickness and pain that had become a part of their daily lives. They learned how to ask for and accept help. We must all try to develop these same caring skills.

How to avoid burnout

As a carer, you have taken on an enormous task. Recognize you will need help – physical, emotional and spiritual – from time to time. The role of primary carer may be entirely new to you. Finding good support for yourself is vitally important. An empty vessel has nothing to give away. Find ways to fill your own vessel so you have *extra* love, blessings, support and solace to pour out for others.

If you have ever flown on an aeroplane, you are familiar with the flight attendant's emergency instructions to put on your own oxygen mask before assisting anyone else. The point is, if you are unconscious from lack of oxygen you cannot help someone else. This concept applies just as well to carers of patients with critical illnesses.

Take care of yourself

Taking care of yourself first is not selfish; it is a necessary requirement for the job! The demands on you in the days ahead will tax you, and to be of the greatest service, you must be strong and well-nourished, both physically and emotionally. I do not tell you this to frighten you, but to warn you. Put on your own 'oxygen mask' first so you are prepared to help someone else. Eat well, get enough sleep, take regular exercise, take breaks and most of all, find people who will support you emotionally while you are doing this important job.

Friends and relatives do not always know what to do or say to either the patient or the carer. This means both you and the patient may feel isolated and alone. This is one of the worst times to feel isolated. Back-up help is essential; let your family know your needs and ask for help. Your honesty will prompt others to come forward to help.

Time for you

In California, USA, a two-day retreat was offered for carers who had been involved for many years in 24-hour care of stroke victims. The retreat, 'A Time to Care for Me', was the first of its kind.

One speaker suggested that carers stay in touch with their feelings and be honest at all times, telling the audience, 'When somebody asks, "How are you doing?" do not answer, "Just fine," if you are snowed under. Instead, admit that times are rough and that you could use a little help or a listening ear for a few minutes.'

Another speaker advised, 'Do not give up your separate existence to take care of another person every minute of every day. Continue to hang on to some separate interests, no matter how small. Any activity of your choosing done merely for yourself will have beneficial results.' Do not think you are being selfish when you do something just for yourself. Think of it as another way to help your loved one.

Some people become completely immersed in their caring role so that they don't have to deal with their emotions. It is important for you to take care of any unfinished business, *before* your loved one dies, so you are not left with unexpressed feelings. It is also a time to begin the grieving process.

Allow yourself to grieve

Bonnie Genevay, a counsellor and consultant who spoke at the retreat, commented, 'Spouses must allow themselves to grieve over the loss of the dreams they shared with their mate – and the loss of touch and recognition from the person with whom they were most intimate. Working through grief frees carers to look toward the future with a sense not only of who they are, but who they can become. Carers are bound to see sorrow when they look ahead, but what about the joys and the potential?'

Recharge yourself

When I was helping care for my dad, Saturdays were my free days. My sister, Barbara, came to help my mother and they both insisted I leave the house. Even if I did not feel like shopping, I still headed over to the mall and strolled around by myself looking in the windows. I sat silently with my thoughts and had lunch, feeling a part of a world where people were bustling around and not thinking about bedpans, pain medication or funerals.

I bought a bright, pink-striped top one Saturday, and whenever I needed a lift I wore it. After my father's death, I continued to think of it as my 'happy shirt' and I put it on whenever I was feeling low.

How to avoid burnout

- Set achievable goals and take one step at a time so you won't be overwhelmed.
- Learn to say no. Don't give beyond your ability to maintain your own emotional and physical well-being.
- Pace yourself. Hurrying through tasks so you can get more done just adds to your stress.
- Anticipate the ways in which your situation will change as your loved one's illness progresses.
- Examine the feelings you have in response to each change so you won't be paralysed by fear or guilt.

After my weekly shopping trips, I returned home refreshed and ready to face another week. One Saturday it was raining fiercely and, much to Barbara's distress, I refused to leave the house. It turned out she was right after all, and I should have taken the break. The following week was rough. I found out for myself how important it is to recharge your batteries so you don't run out of energy.

Express emotions

Another way to avoid burnout is to find a safe place to cry. Tears can express emotions in a way words cannot. Shakespeare wrote, 'To weep is to make less the depth of grief.' Tears are a soothing release and not to be feared or dreaded. Cry with a friend if possible; crying alone denies you the opportunity to be comforted.

In addition to releasing stress by crying, go to a movie, rent a lighthearted video and have a good laugh. There is nothing wrong with taking a 'laugh-break'. The heart can only stand so much suffering and sadness. Allow yourself some relief and respite.

Accept help

Let friends console you when you need consolation. This is not a time to keep a stiff upper lip or go it alone. This is a time to admit you need help, both physical and emotional. Do not neglect either one! Keep up your strength and good spirits. Eat well and exercise daily, no matter how minimal it may be. (A brisk walk around the block is often enough to make you feel better.) Get enough sleep – even if it has to be in snatches instead of in eight-hour blocks, or call in reinforcements so you can get an uninterrupted night's sleep from time to time.

For a change in routine, invite visitors over for yourself. Take time to read or be alone, too. Admit when you feel lousy and overburdened. The less stressed you are, the better support you can offer the patient. Treat yourself to a gift of flowers or a foamy bubble bath from time to time – you deserve it!

Write

Just as talking and listening are effective ways to lower your stress level, so is writing – for both you and your patient. Sometimes it's easier to write down what you feel than it is to say it out loud. You may write just for your eyes only or for others to read.

Keep a daily journal. A journal can help you clarify thoughts and put feelings into proper perspective. Words on paper help keep you on solid ground when everything else is shaky. From time to time, go back and read earlier entries – you'll see the progress you've made and you'll find it helps you make decisions. You can often work out feelings of anger, guilt or frustration through writing in a journal.

Write letters. It's a way of expressing yourself when you find you can't do it face to face. Letters can convey news of your loved one's illness, or request assistance or support when you find it too difficult to do so in person.

If it is difficult for you to talk about personal matters or to express yourself, don't hesitate to make use of these effective writing tools.

Network for support

Another important way to avoid burnout is to network. The dictionary defines 'network' as a series of cords or wires that cross at regular intervals and are knotted or secured at the crossings. You will need people intertwined in your life at regular intervals to make you more secure and replenish your inner resources. Use your telephone or computer to network. Find and obtain all the support you can from information hotlines, individual illness hotlines, support hotlines and websites.

Support groups and information

Check the newspaper for support groups for carers and attend one if possible. The Imperial Cancer Research Fund and the Terrence Higgins Trust are prominent among organizations which sponsor support groups for patients and carers. Talk to social workers and hospice-team members for referrals. If the patient has cancer, telephone your local branch and obtain information on that particular illness. If possible, visit the local office and pick up reading material and resource information that pertains to the illness. I recently searched for materials about cancer on a website, and found an individual site for each particular type of cancer with suggested reading material, chat rooms and hospice referrals. Refer to the resource list on page 121 for more organizations that can help. Your local surgery may have pamphlets with helpful additional information.

Extra help

What services are available from local hospitals, meals on wheels and your local authority? Talk to hospice organizations. If you are a member of a church, notify them of your situation and find out if they can offer help.

Take advantage of available assistance and don't be too proud to ask for help. There will come a time when you can return the good favour; let others help you now, when you need it. Good support can make all the difference to you and to the person for whom you provide care.

5

Caring for the patient

Anyone caring for a person who is terminally ill is likely to experience the same feelings about the illness that the patient experiences. Experts have defined these stages as shock, anger, denial, bargaining, depression, guilt and finally acceptance.

People experience the stages with different intensities and not always in the same sequence. Consider these stages normal as long as one stage does not continue for a long period of time, cause suicidal tendencies, result in extreme depression, or cause the person to harm himself or others.

Honest communication

You and the patient can work out these feelings together by being open and understanding. A terminal prognosis is a heavy burden to carry. Allow the patient to hand over some of the burden to you by letting them express how they feel so they can move ahead more freely. The birth process is easier if the mother prepares properly by exercising, learning special breathing techniques and has a loving partner to assist her. Dying is likewise less difficult for the patient with proper preparation and a loving 'partner' to hold their hand and encourage them.

Talking and writing are two ways to prepare for the end of life. Because each person is unique, find the means that best serves your situation and pursue it. Let the patient know you are a loving partner and that they will not be travelling alone in this new, unfamiliar territory.

Honest communication between you and the patient is crucial. Both you and the patient need to make your needs known and to speak from your hearts.

The diagnosis

Honesty begins with the diagnosis. The patient needs someone to explain exactly what is going on medically and what the options are. When radiation, chemotherapy or surgery have failed to curtail the disease, it is time for someone to be truthful. If the doctor has not done this, that job is up to someone else.

Years ago a study was done of terminal patients to find out if they would have preferred being informed about the seriousness of their illness from the very beginning. Almost every patient agreed they wanted as much time as possible to come to terms with the terminal diagnosis. I questioned our hospice patients on the same subject and the majority conveyed to me they would have been better off if their doctor had been honest with them at the outset.

Treatment

To receive hospice care, patients have to be aware that their prognosis may be only a few months or weeks, and they need a doctor's referral. Sometimes a referral is difficult to obtain. Doctors, especially oncologists, are trained to cure, and they do not like to say there is nothing more that can be done medically. It is often up to the patient or their carer to ask the following questions:

- Will this treatment arrest the disease or put it into remission?
- Is there a possible cure?
- Is there only a slim chance that it will help at all?
- What are the odds of a complete cure?
- Is it time to think about hospice care?

The patient may have to say, 'Please stop treatment. I want to enjoy whatever time is left.' You and the patient may have to request hospice care, and if the oncologist or specialist is not in favour of it, you may have to go back to your original family doctor and explain the situation. Pursue the issue if you feel strongly about it.

Talking about death

A patient who signs the papers for admittance into hospice care knows that they are not expected to live very long. When I was working in hospice, I often found families did not discuss death openly. Frequently it fell to me to open the discussion. I never found a patient who was *not* actively thinking about dying. When I approached the topic, the usual response was one of gratitude – at last the patient could talk openly with someone about their impending death.

Not talking about death takes more energy than accepting the truth. It is exhausting for a person who is sick to keep up a brave front. Pretending everything will be all right wastes what little energy is left. When I approached my patients, they were relieved to talk about what needed to be done before they died. Many patients told me they were more stressed when they were wondering about their prognosis than after they were told they were terminally ill and further treatment would be useless. They *wanted* to talk openly about their concerns and their future.

An opportunity

It's cruel to deny loved ones the opportunity to tie up loose ends and say a final 'I love you'. It is unfair to deny the truth and cheat terminally ill patients out of preparing for one of the most important events in their lives. Don't try to protect your loved ones from what might actually ease their mind.

Helen was a dear, sweet 86-year-old woman who had lived a full happy life. She had been diagnosed with pancreatic cancer and was being cared for on hospice service by her two daughters. Although Helen had signed the admittance papers, our staff did not feel Helen knew she was terminal. They sent me to talk with the family.

I met with the daughters first and they told me that their mother, Helen, would not eat anything. They were overcome with concern and wanted my suggestions for ways to get her to eat. I went over the entire hospice theory in detail again, and stressed that the main goals were to keep the patient happy and comfortable. It was not necessary for her to eat.

'This is a time when you need to relax and just enjoy special moments with your mother. It is no longer a time for trying to cure her. Just sit quietly and hold her hand and love her,' I said. Then I went in to see Helen.

'I'm from the hospice organization,' I told her.

'Are you here to make me better?' she asked.

I took a deep breath. 'You may not be going to get better this time,' I said and I took hold of her hand.

'You think I might be going home to be with the Lord?' she asked.

'Yes, it might be time,' I answered with tears in my eyes.

'Thank you, thank you, honey, for coming and telling me that!' She smiled and patted my hand. 'Does that mean I don't have to eat anymore?'

'That's exactly what it means,' I told her.

'Do my daughters know?'

Always a mother, I thought.

Her relief was apparent. Now she could simply relax. She no longer had to pretend she was going to get well, and she didn't have to force herself to eat. I had given her a whole new perspective on her remaining days and opened the channels of communication with her daughters. My following visits were productive as I watched this family lovingly and gently ease Helen home.

I have mentioned previously that a terminal diagnosis can be thought of as a final gift. It allows for a natural slow-down, a time to put all affairs, emotional and spiritual, in order. It provides time for mending relationships and for spiritual growth that is not available with a sudden, unexpected death. Tim Brooker sums it up perfectly in his book *Signs of Life*. He writes that most people say that they would prefer to die quickly.

If people think about their own death at all, they are likely to want something swift and painless. When someone dies suddenly, with no warning, they do not have to think about their death, plan for it or fear it. There is no time for reflection; it simply happens and is over. In some ways, wishing for a quick death is a form of denial. To know in advance that death is approaching, and facing the fear, provides great opportunities. The remaining time is often one of profound love and improved relationships. As the carer, you have been given the chance to participate in this most valuable and enriching time with the patient. Do not avoid it; make the most of it.

Open the door

The first time you approach the subject of death is the most difficult. Once the door has been opened and you see what a welcome guest the subject is, you won't hesitate to continue to talk about it. I was often surprised by the change in demeanour of my patients when I spoke about death with them. They would smile or sigh with relief, and usually say, 'Thank you. I've been waiting to talk about this with someone.'

At first it may be difficult to talk about the fact that time may be limited. To be open about a terminal illness does not indicate resignation; it is merely preparation. Gently approach the subject by using the words 'if' and 'may'. I make statements such as, 'If you don't get well, what are your wishes?' 'Your illness may be in the last stages.' We never know, for sure, when a miracle might come. Therefore, even though all the evidence points away from a recovery, we must hold on to hope.

I saw two such miracles in six years. Two people, who by all medical standards should not be walking around, are living productive lives today. These were hospice patients who seemed to be mere days from death's door, yet they recovered. As a result, I know never to give up hope.

81

Listening skills

Instead of asking the patient, 'How are you feeling?' ask, 'What are you feeling?' and be prepared to listen. Most of good communication is good listening. The greatest gift you can give the patient is to be a good listener.

I was told that people have two ears and one mouth because they are supposed to listen twice as much as they speak. Good advice, but not especially easy to follow. Being a good listener does not come naturally to most people. It is a skill learned from constant practice. Anyone who wants to help a person who is hurting needs to learn active, reflective, effective, creative and sensitive listening skills.

What to say

Sometimes nothing is harder to do than simply listen. As the friend or loved one of a critically ill person, you know how painful it is to listen as doubts and fears, anger and frustration are revealed. Yet listening is the most compassionate gift you can offer. To shut the door by responding uncomfortably with phrases such as, 'Everything will be fine', or 'Try not to think about it', do not help. Repeating empty clichés only isolates the patient further.

Instead, use proven ways to show you care. When you hear distress in the patient's voice, address it immediately. Offer help and try to find solutions to the immediate problems. Also offer spiritual support to the patient if appropriate.

In addition to working in hospice, I also led a number of bereavement support groups. From that experience, I wrote a book on grief called *How Can I Help?* Many of the same listening skills that are helpful in supporting people who are grieving can help you support your loved one.

Studies show that one of the best ways to work through grief is to talk about it. Patients with life-threatening illnesses are grieving the loss of life on earth. They need friends to listen as they talk through their grief.

Active listening

Active listening is a communication technique in which the listener does not interfere with the speaker's message. It means listening to what is being said without interjecting your own judgements, advice or analysis. Active listening is a highly effective tool for comprehension of what you are told. It has the added advantage of being a useful way to help others clarify their feelings.

Active listening encourages the speaker to expand on the problem. You may respond with a statement such as, 'Yes, go on,' 'Tell me more about that,' or a nod of the head to show interest.

When a person has trouble clarifying his or her thoughts, you can respond with, 'Then this is the problem as you see it,' and repeat the information you heard, paraphrasing. If your assumptions are incorrect, the speaker can correct you, which also helps the speaker clarify his or her thoughts. Active listening keeps the lines of communication open. It helps individuals express their feelings by putting them into words. A listener who shows shock, is judgemental, condemns or gives advice stifles further sharing. It is better to show acceptance, letting the speaker know you are there in a supportive capacity.

Reflective listening

Reflective listening goes a step further. The listener paraphrases or 'reflects' back what has just been said, to assure the speaker he or she has been heard correctly. For example, the speaker might say, 'I'm too tired to even think straight.' This is paraphrased back by the listener as, 'It sounds to me like you are feeling overwhelmed and exhausted.' Another example, 'I don't know what to do. There are too many decisions to make,' can be paraphrased as, 'You must be feeling quite pressured over this situation.'

This is not merely being an echo. Reflective listening lets speakers know you heard what was said, affirms you have understood correctly and allows them to form their next thought without being interrupted. When you listen this way you notice details that will help you help the speaker.

Effective listening

Effective listening involves hearing the tone of voice the speaker is using: 'I can hear that this situation makes you angry' or 'You must be feeling very helpless about this problem.' Statements like these allow the speaker to expand on the idea and, perhaps, find a possible solution. Giving advice is generally not helpful to a person who is agonizing over a situation. It is likely to add more confusion to an already stressful situation.

Sensitive listening

Sensitive listening is necessary at all times and in all situations. It involves your full attention. You express sensitive listening with body language, eye contact, appropriate touching and posture. You sit down in a room instead of standing – close enough to touch if contact seems necessary. Do not sit behind a desk, for example, because that puts a barrier between you and the speaker.

Listening sensitively means focusing on the thoughts and feelings that the speaker expresses rather than on your own. Eye contact is vitally important. Have you ever shared an innermost thought with someone who was looking around the room? That sends the message that the listener is looking for something more interesting to do. To listen in a sensitive way, give your undivided attention to the speaker and respond in an appropriate manner.

When listening with sensitivity, remember that feelings are neither good or bad, they just *are*. Delete the phrase 'You shouldn't feel that way' from your vocabulary. It is judgemental and a conversation-stopper. If you show shock, disgust or become defensive, it slams the door to further sharing. The patient gets the message that you are unable to handle what is going on and will spare you from further confrontations with the truth. This can make the patient feel isolated and may result in depression. Instead, use a loving response when feelings are shared – nod and make eye contact while you try to understand.

Body language

Make physical contact with speakers when they pour out their hearts. Show you can accept their anger, pain and the depth of their feelings without being devastated too. Be the rock your loved ones can grab when they are battered by waves of despair.

If you avoid eye contact, fold your arms or lean away from a person, you are using body language that expresses a wish to withdraw from the speaker. Instead, reflect back your feelings in a simple way that lets the person know you have heard what was said. Paraphrasing is one technique; good body language is another.

As you listen, reach out and touch the patient at the proper times. Holding a hand or putting an arm around a person who is trying to say something gut-wrenching gives them the courage to express themselves more fully. The speaker can physically feel your support. In addition, asking questions shows you are interested and concerned. To develop a successful exchange of ideas, be creative!

Ask questions

Creative, sensitive listening interspersed with questions can be the most helpful tool you have to offer people who are terminally ill. It gives them the chance to vent the anger and confusion they feel. It helps them form plans for the future. It banishes lonely or abandoned feelings. And it comforts, giving the reassurance that someone *does* care. I once heard someone say, 'Questions are like the banks of a river; they channel the flow of the conversation.' Ask questions to bridge gaps in conversation. It shows you care. Do not ask invasive or rude questions, of course, but ones that show you are truly interested in what matters to the other person.

Share life experiences

This might be the perfect time to encourage the patient to share his life experiences. Hospice volunteers call it taking walks down memory lane. They begin by asking questions about photographs displayed in the home. Family members can suggest getting out old photographs and asking questions about the patient's childhood. Stories shared at the end of life are priceless. They are often pieces of family history that might be otherwise lost forever.

Tim Brooker writes in *Signs of Life* that this process of recollection, 'often called a Life Review, is the subject of a certain amount of study these days ... In [my mother's] case, it seemed to me that we were giving her permission to roam the length and breadth of her life and make sure that there was nothing of value in it that she might have lost or forgotten, and time and again the impish schoolgirl broke through, as if the process were a gathering, or perhaps a rediscovery, of her spirit.' What a wonderful opportunity for families! Take advantage of this time of inactivity and have a final, meaningful visit, filled with affection and shared memories.

Location of care

At some point, it is necessary to discuss home care and hospital care with the patient. Items to be considered in this decision are:

- What is the patient's first choice?
- Are there one or two willing full-time carers available?
- What financial resources are available?
- Is quantity or quality of life most important?
- How does the patient feel about resuscitation and life-support machines?
- How about artificial feeding and hydration?
- What about antibiotics for pneumonia or unrelated illnesses?

- Is outside help such as a social worker, therapist or hospice necessary and available?

Hospital care

If your loved one chooses to be hospitalized, look into the most convenient, suitable facility available. Check all possible choices and gather all the facts before making decisions. Hospital or convalescent care is required when no full-time carer is available, and patients reach a point where they cannot care for themselves.

The dignity of the patient must be a high priority, taking second place only to safety. Never make plans without consulting the patient and never speak down to them. Let them do all they can for themselves and put them in charge of decision-making and choices. As a carer, do only what is necessary at each step. As the illness progresses, your amount of involvement increases. Do not take command until it is requested or obviously needed.

Even when a patient is hospitalized, it is a good idea to have someone visit the patient frequently. The hospital staff are often so busy with emergencies that they cannot tend to simple tasks like filling a jug with fresh water. Patients fare better when a concerned person is present to help with personal needs.

Hospitals can be lonely places and even short visits from caring persons can lift the spirits. Small, thoughtful gifts like lip balm, hand lotion or a magazine are often appreciated more than flowers.

Home care

A Gallup survey in 1996 indicated that nine out of ten people would rather die at home – and a majority expressed interest in hospice care. To die at home is to die surrounded by love. It is a time of intense closeness that can bring a family together as nothing else can. Relationships can be mended, love can be reinforced, and the patient can gain strength and encouragement from loved ones. In addition, patients are usually more content and feel better physically at home.

Schedules

When patients are being cared for at home, they are free from the anxiety of unfamiliar schedules and unfamiliar faces. At home, the schedule can be set with the patient's comfort in mind. There is a continuity of care that the patient can help choose. The patient receives tender care from people who knew them prior to their illness, which helps restore emotional balance at a time when everything else seems out of balance. At the same time, carers benefit from the opportunity to observe the end of a life at close range and to learn from it as they assist in the process.

One of my fondest memories involves my mother in her final days. I went to be with her in her home when she was discharged from the hospital. While in the hospital, she got her days and nights mixed up. She slept most of the first day at home and I confidently thought, 'Piece of cake!' I got everything in order around the house, talked with the hospice team and notified relatives of her current condition.

Just as I was falling asleep around midnight, Mom summoned me by banging the spoon we had tied to her bed rail. I dragged myself into her room with only one eye open. As soon as Mom saw me, her face lit up and with her usual cheerfulness, she said, 'Good morning. What's for breakfast?'

Now it was no longer a piece of cake! She would not believe it was midnight, and did not especially care, because she was hungry and wide awake. I pacified her with a glass of milk and some cookies, and I sat on her bed and shared her midnight snack. We laughed and talked and shared some beautiful memories. Then I turned out the light and returned to bed with a smile on my face.

However, the smile lasted only until I was snuggled under the blankets and I again heard Mom's summons. This time I felt like I was dragging an extra 50 pounds on my back as I approached her room. The previous scenario was repeated. 'Good morning,' she said spryly and cheerfully. Again, she would not believe it was the middle of the night, but this time I could not pacify her with milk and cookies. I made her breakfast and spent the next day keeping her awake to get her on a better schedule.

I often picture her sweet, cheerful face, aglow with finding me in her room and her sweet 'Good mornings!' Even in her final illness, my mother built bridges of love that would carry me across troubled waters. It has been years now, but I can recall it clearly, and feel she is still with me for rare and precious moments. I would have missed this opportunity if I had not been caring for her in her home.

Sharing the dying process

When Mom chose to die at home, she gave permission to her family to share her dying process. Watching her took away any fear I might have had about death. It left my family feeling rewarded for the care we had given my mother, and she felt much more content in her own home.

It takes great reserves of energy to care for a terminal patient around the clock; however, the compensations do outweigh the fatigue. No experience is more intimate than being with someone as they face the end of life. To be able to share in that private time, and to encourage a loved one to let go gently, knits families closer together than almost any other situation.

Sharing the caregiving responsibilities

If the patient wants to be at home, but no full-time carer is available, it is sometimes possible to set up shifts of numerous carers or to hire help. I have seen an ex-wife come back home to care for a patient. I have seen neighbours each take over caring responsibilities for one day a week. I have seen relatives travel from out of town and each stay one week during the months of illness. I have seen a son from halfway across the world return home to care for his mother. Ask for help! You will not receive it until you tell loved ones there is a need.

Supplies for home care

It is as easy to learn to care for a person who is ill as it is to learn to care for a newborn. Both jobs require practice, patience and lots of love. Both chores seem unsurmountable at first, but they become easier, and finally indescribably rewarding.

If the patient chooses to be cared for at home, you'll need certain items on hand for comfort of the patient and for your ease. Medical skills and training are not necessary. Many helpful books are available that go into great detail on ways to set up a 'home hospital' and care for a patient at home. The following list will help you set up a sick room properly and offers basic suggestions for getting started.

- Hospital beds are more comfortable for most patients and make the care easier for nurses and family members. Place the bed in a central, cheerful location, such as the family room.
- Place a bell or other means of summoning help close to the bed. An inexpensive baby monitor can be quite helpful.
- A jug of water or juice should be within easy reach on a nightstand or a special rollaway table near the bed.
- An 'egg box' mattress pad helps prevent bedsores. Frequent turning and repositioning are also necessary.
- Provide lots of extra pillows for propping or cushioning sensitive areas.
- A cassette recorder close to the bed allows the patient to listen to

favourite music or tape messages, especially during the long night-time hours.

- Inspirational reading material should be close at hand for lonely times.
- Time-honoured remedies such as hot tea, heating pads and hot-water bottles are still quite effective, especially to relieve anxiety. Often, just changing from one position to another is distracting enough to relieve breathing problems caused by stress.
- Frequent massages and applying lotion or oil to keep skin in good condition can be both soothing and relaxing.
- Do not force food. It is not always necessary for the patient to eat.
- Bowel movements may become sluggish due to pain medication or inactivity. Inform nurses of the status.
- If the patient has difficulty swallowing, liquids can be given with a large syringe specially made for that purpose. If the patient can drink from a glass, special no-spill cups with spouted lids work well.

Physical care

The physical care of the patient involves many factors. The best way to proceed is with good communication with the patient and either a handbook on patient care or help from medically trained personnel.

Nutrition

Nutrition and mealtimes can be among the most distressing aspects of the job unless the carer understands the old rules about eating and nutrition no longer apply. Even in the early stages the patient may have little or no appetite as a result of the illness or medical treatment and may resist eating. It is natural for carers to feel inadequate when they are unable to nourish a loved one. In turn, the patient feels guilty for upsetting the carer by not eating.

Offering food

Often one of the greatest joys shared by loved ones is eating together. To give up shared delights is difficult. For carers to eat alone in the next room, while they think their loved one is starving, is rough. In my hospice work, no matter how often the nurses and I told the patient and carer that it was not necessary to eat, they had trouble letting go of the idea. In a typical situation, the wife would coax and bribe her husband until he agreed to eat. Even if he only ate a bite or two, the wife was happy. This situation made extra work for the wife and upset her husband.

This is the time when good communication skills can help. Offer food, but make it clear it is not necessary for the patient to eat. A better solution is to say, 'I'll be happy to cook whatever you have a taste for, if you feel like eating.' Possibly suggest an item or two that may have been satisfying in the past, but make it clear you won't be upset if the patient cannot eat.

When food is no longer necessary

Eventually, the time will come when the patient's body no longer needs or wants food. Try not to make the patient feel guilty for not eating and do not take the refusal of food personally. Offer liquids frequently; sports bottles with straws attached to the lids work well. I find that if I put the water bottle in the freezer just long enough to let some ice form, it stays cool much longer. Look for cups with spill-proof tops. Let the patient choose what works best. Using a straw may also help. Frozen pops and slushy drinks often appeal to people who otherwise find food unappealing. Experiment, but don't pressure the patient.

When nothing else sounds appealing, small cubes of ice may be used to prevent dehydration. Offer them frequently. At some point, the patient will even refuse ice cubes and liquids. If their mouth becomes dry and uncomfortable, a moist flannel can be sucked on. Water can be squirted into the mouth with a large syringe made for that purpose if the patient requests liquid, but is unable to drink. Never put anything into the mouth of a comatose or unconscious person.

Nature, knowing what is best, gradually shuts down a body's systems. Do not feel guilty for not feeding or giving drinks to a patient who no longer desires them.

Elimination

The elimination of urine and stool is something most of us take for granted until the system stops working properly or a person cannot get to the toilet of their own accord. Sickroom supply services have equipment to make elimination easier. One handy item is a bedside commode that can be placed near the bed. These commodes have a removable part for easy disposal and cleaning. You can help the patient move from the bed to the commode and back again, unless you are much smaller and weaker than the patient. If this is the case, you can obtain various types of bedpans and urinals that can be used in the bed.

Your community nurse can tell you how to use the devices and explain the differences among them. Also available are pads to place under the patient to keep sheets clean. A broad range of disposable undergarments meet almost any need when the patient no longer can get to the bedside commode or use a bedpan.

Allowing privacy

Allow the patient as much privacy as possible when using the commode. Once the patient is seated, leave the room, if possible, and suggest that they call when they need you. Have toilet paper handy and let the patient do as much for themselves as possible.

When a bedpan is used, sprinkle it with talcum powder first to help it slide under the patient more easily. Again, leave the patient alone to use it unless you are afraid of potential injury.

These issues are all delicate and need to be handled openly and honestly. The patient must not feel a burden, and you have to be able to be straightforward in dealing with incontinence and bedpans. Most people feel awkward at first, but with a little humour and lots of tenderness, everyone gets through it without a loss of dignity for the patient.

Changes in elimination

When food intake decreases, elimination also decreases. Do not be too concerned if the patient does not have a bowel movement every day. As long as the patient is comfortable and does not feel constipated, it is not a problem. Stool softeners are often prescribed to keep the bowel movements softer when food intake is low. If the patient experiences any distress because of the lack of a bowel movement, tell the medical team. Do not self-treat constipation with over-the-counter remedies.

Urine production decreases as liquid consumption decreases, and it may be darker in colour. Do not be concerned unless blood is present or urination ceases completely. Do report to someone on the medical team any burning or unusual sensation the patient may feel while urinating.

Other supplies and sanitation

Moist towelettes have many uses in the sickroom, as do plastic gloves when dealing with bodily waste. Be cautious of sanitation when disposing of soiled garments and items. Incontinence pads, soiled bed pads, used plastic gloves, cotton swabs and tissues should be double-bagged before being put out with the rubbish. Plastic bags reduce odours and contamination. Even when illnesses are not contagious, it is still necessary to remember proper sanitary conditions.

I hesitate to write about plastic bags, nursing pads and disposable undergarments, because they are not completely biodegradable. However, these items are needed only temporarily. Continual progress is being made to make these products biodegradable. I suggest you use recycled plastic bags whenever possible. I have seen families save every plastic bag that came into their home, even the bags that hold bread and frozen vegetables, and re-use them for other purposes. Be creative, but don't sacrifice proper sanitation.

Pain medication

Good pain control is essential. If a patient is uncomfortable, so are you. Report increased pain to the doctor or nurse and keep them informed until it is under control. Do not feel you are being a pest! The doctor has no way of knowing the patient is suffering unless you say so.

Talking about pain

A hospice volunteer once reported to me that her patient was suffering terribly. One day when the volunteer visited the patient, the patient moaned and rocked with pain. The volunteer had been there only a short time when the hospice nurse arrived. The patient brightened, put on her company manners, and responded that she was 'just fine'. After the nurse had taken her vital statistics, written her report and departed, the volunteer asked the patient why she had not told the nurse about her pain.

'I hate to sound like a whiner', was her response.

Cancer and pain

Almost 50 per cent of terminal cancer patients have little or no pain even without prescription drugs. Cancer is not necessarily a painful disease, but many people aren't aware of that fact. When pain is connected with a particular type of cancer, it is almost always controllable – but only if a medical professional is aware of it.

Fortunately, the volunteer reported the incident to me and I took it back to the nursing staff. The nurse returned to the patient's house and asked the patient point-blank if she was having pain. The real story finally came out. The nurse called the doctor and the medication was changed. Two days later, the patient was pain-free and able to visit with relatives who had arrived from out of town.

When asked, most terminal patients say they are more afraid of the *process* of dying than of death. They fear an agonizing death, the loss of dignity or the loss of mental stability. Offer encouragement and reassurances that you are there to make the process as easy as possible. Exercise every possible means to maintain the patient's dignity and self-respect.

You and the patient have the right to ask for increased doses or a change in medication. Doctors rightfully assume that everything is fine unless you report otherwise. They do not want their patients suffering needlessly. Many pain medications on the market can be given alone or in conjunction with others to give the best relief with the fewest side effects. Don't hesitate to ask for better pain relief for the patient. As the illness progresses, doctors expect that pain patterns may change. Keep the medical team up to date!

Addiction

Whenever large doses of narcotic drugs are discussed, there is concern about addiction. I once heard a hospice nurse sum it up this way: 'We don't fear addiction with terminal patients. We give them as much medication as they need. If a miracle were to occur and they got well, the pain would cease. With no pain, there would no longer be a need for the drug and the dependency would be easy to reverse.' Hospice workers generally agree that the fear of addiction with terminal cases is not as great as the need for comfort. Remember you are *caring* for these patients, not *curing* them. The most caring thing you can do is to spare suffering.

Home remedies

Tried and tested comfort remedies still work today. When I feel down, a cup of hot tea with milk soothes me, not because of any medicinal value, but because my mother served me hot tea with milk whenever I was upset as a child. Most families have tricks like these they can pull off a back shelf. Use a wide variety of methods to alleviate pain.

Aromatherapy

Appeal to the sense of smell to enhance feelings of tranquillity. Aromatherapy is popular these days and a wide variety of products exist. Scented candles, potpourri, plug-in room deodorizers and even scented oils that can be placed in special holders on your light bulbs are easy to find. Certain fragrances may evoke happy memories in your household. Take advantage of these items and use them to help promote a soothing atmosphere.

A homemade ice bag

The most convenient and least expensive ice bag is a frozen bag of peas wrapped in a towel. It has just enough weight and flexibility to mould itself to the body and stays frozen for a considerable time. Frozen peas cost less than ice bags or cold packs from the chemist and they can be refrozen. When my doctor told me about this convenient 'ice bag', she reminded me to write 'not for human consumption' on the outside of the bag so that the peas would not be mistakenly eaten after being defrosted and refrozen numerous times. I gave her a sly grin and asked, 'Would "Do not eat" work?' However you choose to say it, mark the bag so the peas will not be eaten.

I was always amazed at the ingenuity in households where I visited hospice patients. In one home, a woman began to bake her own bread just so her husband could enjoy the fresh, almost forgotten fragrance from his happy childhood. Another family had cinnamon sticks boiling on the stove all day long simply for the scent. Spices are familiar odours that often recall happy holiday seasons. One patient loved oranges, but could no longer eat them, so the family sliced them and placed them near her bed simply for her to smell. When experimenting with aromas, check with the patient first. Even if pizza used to be the patient's favourite dish, its strong, distinct odour may now bring on nausea.

A *helping hand*

Just as odours can soothe, so can music. Often these 'props' are so effective at bringing relief and consolation that pain medication can be decreased. Heating pads, ice bags, massages with warm lotion or oil are all helpful relaxation tools.

About suicide and euthanasia

Death should come naturally, and even slowly, believes Dr Ira Byock, a supporter of laws banning doctor-assisted suicide – a matter of international medical and ethical concern. Dr Byock, president of the

American Academy of Hospice and Palliative Medicine, is devoted to compassionate care for people in their final stage of life.

He, along with many others, feels we should be helping people die *better*, not quicker. Just as doctors should not use aggressive treatment when there is no hope for a cure, they should not hasten death before it comes naturally.

Depression

When a patient is terminally ill, depression is often on the scene. If depression becomes extreme, the patient may become discouraged enough to ask for assistance or permission to commit suicide. I have occasionally encountered this situation.

Every time, I had a gut feeling that the patient simply needed reassurance from loved ones that he or she was not an overwhelming burden or financial drain. I spoke with loved ones and carers, explaining the situation and my thoughts about it. In each case, after the carer reassured the patient that he was needed and loved and was *not* a burden, the patient stopped talking about suicide and the crisis passed.

A terminal patient may feel unproductive because of incapacities, but even in dire illness, personal growth is continuing and life has a purpose. The growth may be spiritual where it cannot be seen, or it may be noticed as little sparks of love and appreciation. To end life unnaturally would interfere with the natural growth process.

Intervention

If your loved one begins to express suicidal thoughts or asks you to help end their life, do not act shocked. Treat the situation with tenderness and openness, and look for underlying causes, such as deep despair. Be especially aware of whether the patient is formulating a specific plan for ending their life. Wishing to commit suicide and actually having a plan for carrying it out are vastly different. Seek professional help and use crisis intervention. Ring the Samaritans.

Look for underlying causes for the crisis. Is the depression a side-effect of new medication? Is treatment for anxiety needed temporarily? Could the pain medication be decreased or increased? Discuss these issues with your medical team. At the same time, show gentle concern for the patient – plan a special family gathering with uplifting music and memory-sharing to lift the patient's spirits.

Lovingly give the patient a reason to hold on until the immediate wish to die recedes. Offer abundant compassion, understanding and encouragement, and seek professional help if you remain concerned.

Most important, do not ignore any mention of suicide; it is usually a cry for help.

Physical contact

One of the best ways to soothe another person is through touch. Cancer is not contagious and neither are many other catastrophic diseases, so do not be afraid to touch or express affection. No person feels more fragile and in need of human contact than one who is fighting a life-threatening illness.

One obstacle to close contact is the hospital bed. As comfortable and as convenient as a hospital bed is, it presents problems with regard to close physical contact. Hospital beds are higher off the floor than a regular bed, and they have side rails. I have found it is virtually impossible to give a hug or kiss when the rails are up. Frequently I see patients in hospital beds with the sides up even when it is not necessary. Unless there is a fear of the patient falling, the bed rails don't have to be up during the day – it isolates the patient needlessly.

I once asked a group of volunteers to do a role-playing exercise. We took turns lying in a bed to see how a patient feels. The rest of the volunteers hovered over the bed from above, as people do with patients. The feeling was one of doom and claustrophobia. It made us all quite aware of the way it must feel to be the patient, and it helped us remember to lower the rails of the bed whenever possible, so we could get close to the patient, preferably at the patient's own level.

I liked to sit on the bed next to my patients so we could hold hands or touch. I often saw dogs and cats on the bed; I figured if they can climb on, so could I. Nevertheless, I always asked permission first and made sure it would not cause the patient discomfort. I was cautious to hug gently, and if I wasn't sure about the level of pain or the location of tender areas, I asked before hugging.

Intimacy

Spouses should remain physically close as long as it is feasible. Sexual expression may have to change, but it does not need to be given up completely. Plan times alone when the patient is feeling well, and if possible, close the door. If the bed is in a central location, you may have to send friends and family out for a few hours so you can have some private time. One family posted a sign on the refrigerator stating, 'Clear the premises every day from 1.00 p.m. to 3.00 p.m. – or else!' It worked.

A patient may feel unattractive due to surgery, weight loss, hair loss or other physical changes. Reassurance and a gentle sense of humour can ease many an awkward moment. In addition to touch, sound and smell can enhance the feelings of sensuality for the patient. Soft music playing in the background makes a hospital setting seem less sterile, just as pleasant aromas enhance the atmosphere. Light a fragrant candle and let the luscious scent permeate the room with the romantic flicker of a candle flame. This is the time to use your imagination and add those special touches that bring about feelings of peace and contentment. Even the darkest hour can be brightened when you are making life more pleasant for the person you love.

When actress Gilda Radner was terminally ill with ovarian cancer, I was surprised to see so many photographs of her with her almost bald head. Ordinarily, I would expect people who work in entertainment to be too vain to allow themselves that type of public exposure. I later read an article by her husband, Gene Wilder, in which he said how cute he thought Gilda looked after her hair loss. He said he loved her 'bean sprouts' of baby-fine hair. Because he assured her it was sexy, she too, was able to accept the situation and not feel self-conscious. You can help your loved one by making light of what may otherwise seem like insurmountable physical changes.

Children's love

I am always amazed that young children accept easily what adults often consider unacceptable. Grandma's bald head, for example, does not shock or distress them. They may ask blunt questions and may want to touch the bald head. When this happens, it lightens the situation for everyone involved.

Grandchildren love to climb in bed with their grandparents for hugs – encourage it! Children learn that people sometimes become ill and incapacitated. The extra love from the children can give the patient a real boost.

Contagious smiles

When her mother-in-law was hospitalized, my daughter Kathy wanted to be with her at the hospital while she waited to be taken into surgery. Because Kathy was still nursing her three-month-old son Andrew, she decided to take him along. It turned out to be a blessing to the entire ward.

At this stage of his life, Andrew did nothing but smile – literally. He smiled at his hands and at his feet; he smiled at his brother and sister, and at any face that came into his view. He was a precious baby who never seemed to cry. As Kathy walked through the hospital 'prep' room, patients were lined up in their beds waiting their turn in the operating theatre. As she passed each bed, the patient's face lit up with a smile.

This struck her as rather unusual until she realized they were merely responding to Andrew. She was holding him in her arms, and he had a smile for each person he passed. Several patients asked to see him closer, simply wanting to touch his little dimpled hands or chubby feet. Andrew was a precious gift and a special comfort to many people that morning.

Teenagers

If there are teenagers in your family they can learn valuable lessons from you. Although they might pretend not to notice, they are watching you carefully and they will copy your actions when they are adults.

When my father was in his final illness, I was out of town for more than a month helping care for him, and I had frequent pangs of guilt. My youngest daughter was preparing for her high school graduation and my eldest daughter was making arrangements for her wedding. I felt I should be at home to support my daughters with the preparations. My wise friend Gerrie eased my guilt when she told me the example I was setting for my children was more important than being available to them.

'You're showing them that responsible adults take care of their elderly parents when they are needed. And that death is a part of life that should be shared, not hidden. They are seeing your priorities and learning a valuable lesson. In ten years, they won't remember who made the telephone call to order the helium balloons for their party, but they *will* remember that you were at your dad's bedside holding his hand as he lay dying.' Now, with ten years' hindsight, I can affirm that Gerrie was right.

Encourage touch

Encourage all visitors, adults and children alike, to touch, hug and sit close to the patient. Let them know it is appreciated and allowed. People can be uncomfortable around illness and unsure of proper behaviour. It may be up to you to set the pace.

An exception to this practice might be the case of patients who have a low tolerance to infection. Let the patient's professional team advise you, so you can be aware and well-informed.

Explaining death to children

Don't shelter children from the reality of the illness and the patient's possible death. Include them in the care and in discussions about the future. By including them, you provide a foundation that will serve them well when death occurs in their adult lives. The more comfortable the adults are with a situation, the more easily their children will adjust to death later in their lives.

Just remember that children under six or seven years old have a difficult time understanding that death is permanent. Television cartoons do nothing to help this concept. Children see people blown to bits and get up and walk around in the next frame. Be careful with your explanations and be available to answer questions.

What to say

Word choice is especially important when explaining death to young children. Avoid euphemisms. Do not say a deceased person has 'gone to sleep', 'is in heaven', 'has become an angel', or that 'God needed them'. These phrases are easily misunderstood and can cause further problems. Dan Schaefer, author of *How Do We Tell the Children?*, suggests telling a child that the person got very sick and the doctors could not fix him. His body stopped working. Children understand when things stop working and cannot be fixed. The fact does not frighten them and is within their realm of recognition. Schaefer's book is a must-read if there are young children involved in your caregiving.

Using props

Terms like 'God' and 'heaven' are difficult enough concepts for adults, let alone children. A must-read is *Go Toward the Light* by Chris Oyler. She writes how her husband, Grant, explained death to their children when they found out their seven-year-old son had AIDS.

Grant used his hand and a glove to explain the difference between the spirit and the body. 'When you were born,' he told his children, 'you were given a body.' Grant put his hand in the glove showing how the spirit now had a body. He wiggled his fingers inside the glove, explaining it was the spirit that gave the body life, just like his hand gave 'life' to the glove.

Chris Oyler explains that her children were fascinated. None of them made a sound. Before proceeding, Grant made sure they truly understood. He paused and studied each of their faces. When you die, he continued, it's as if the body just slips off again. He removed the glove from his hand and placed it on the table in front of the boys. They stared at the lifeless object.

Then he wiggled his fingers and explained that our bodies may die, but our spirits never die. Our spirits live forever. Using a visual aid, like a hand and glove, while explaining in words a child can understand, is quite effective.

Children and funerals

Children should not be shielded from funerals or final rites. They are times of closure for children as well as adults and serve a genuine purpose. When children are included, they are better able to understand the finality of death. Encourage young people to place a flower on the grave, a note in the coffin or perform some other ritual as their own personal part in the ceremony. It can be a meaningful experience and part of healthy growth. Children are more troubled by being excluded than they are by participating. Just be sure not to force a reluctant child into anything. Explain thoroughly what is going on and then let them choose if they wish to participate.

Watch children's behaviour

Children normally adjust well to both the process of dying and death if they are included in the process. Keep the channels of communication open so they feel comfortable expressing fears and asking questions. Watch for these simple signs that could indicate there is trouble brewing.

- *Notice sudden personality changes.* Something may be troubling the child that he or she is unable to express. Watch for an outgoing child who suddenly begins to spend a lot of time alone, or a shy child who becomes disruptive.
- *Observe eating and sleeping habits.* Unexplained changes in eating or sleeping patterns, or nightmares could indicate unresolved issues that need to be discussed.
- *Watch for changes in school work or behaviour.* Inform teachers of the home situation so they can notify you if there are drastic changes at school.
- *Listen for obsessive concern over their own health.* A discussion on details of the illness can dispel any fears about a child's personal health.
- *Crying easily or being unusually stoic can indicate problems.* These can be signs of unresolved anger or guilt, or feelings that need to be expressed and given attention.

If the child shows any of these signs, talk with the child to find out what is going on. Seek professional help if you feel it is necessary. Above all, be open and honest with any children who are involved. When children are left out or lied to, they suffer much more than when they know what to expect. Be available to answer questions.

Children often feel a parent's illness is some kind of punishment for something they thought, said or did. Reassure them that illness occurs randomly and is nobody's fault. Do prepare children for impending death so it doesn't shock them when the time comes, and also so they can give and receive love while there is time. Children are amazingly resilient and deserve the same considerations as adults. They can benefit from anticipatory grief just as adults can.

Anticipatory grief

When a death occurs suddenly, loved ones have no opportunity to prepare themselves. The shock and suffering, along with any unfinished business, makes the process of grief almost unbearable.

The feelings you are experiencing now – the anguish, the agony, the anger, the yearning and the depression – have been given the name of *anticipatory grief*. Being able to discuss the possibility of death with the patient before the time comes makes the adjustment afterwards easier. You will have started down the road of bereavement and already begun the grief process.

Living with a terminal prognosis of a loved one is painful. It is like taking an unplanned journey down an unfamiliar path, with many jogs in the road. Each jog involves a major decision as you continue down the road. You are expected to have great reserves of love, energy and endurance as you walk towards an unknown destination. Will there be a miracle along the way? Will the illness make the journey longer than expected or will you be left alone very soon?

Living a person who is terminally ill forces you to face issues you may feel unprepared to think about. Your choices are limited; your feelings are in constant turmoil. Yet, this can be a special time, filled with tender moments and rewards of knowing you have taken on one of the most important tasks in life.

A final gift

In the midst of stumbling along this unchosen path, there is one small consolation: you have been given a final gift of time to adapt to this drastic change. With advance warning, you have an opportunity to make plans, help get legal issues in order and find out about the patient's wishes for final arrangements. You have been given the chance to say goodbye, to express your love, to tie up loose ends and to make amends.

6

Final arrangements

Final arrangements can be made prior to a death. Many terminally ill patients choose to make their own arrangements or to be actively involved in the plans. This requires great delicacy and should be handled carefully. If you have a hospice organization caring for the patient, they can approach the topic and open the discussion.

The patient's wishes

If you are dealing with the patient without the support of hospice, you may want to ask a suitable person, such as a pastor or a friend who is comfortable discussing death, for help. You can deal with the subject in general terms or in a completely open way, depending on whether the patient has reached acceptance or is still partially in denial of the situation.

Opening the discussion

A discussion of legal matters often evolves into a discussion of final arrangements. Read the section on legal matters on pages 53–5 and go over it with the patient. Put paperwork in order, note insurance policy numbers and put military discharge papers and national health insurance certificates in an accessible place.

Another way to open the discussion on final arrangements is to talk about personal items. Ask, 'Is there any item you would want someone in particular to have, in case you don't get well?' If the patient seems interested in this topic, suggest starting a list so there will be no confusion or mistakes. Some people choose to present the gifts themselves prior to their death. This can be a lovely gesture and provides both giver and receiver great pleasure (see pages 51–3).

Consider the best way to discuss final arrangements. Choose an approach that is most suitable in your situation. Pick a time when the patient is comfortable and alert and approach the subject gently. Take care not to leave the patient without hope. Make it clear this discussion is taking place *in the event* the patient does not have a miraculous recovery. Do not force the conversation if the patient seems hesitant about discussing his own final arrangements.

Indirect approaches

Even when the patient is in denial, you can use back-door approaches to obtain information. You can ask, in general terms, if they think cremation is preferable to burial. You can ask about special songs, religious readings, soloists and pastors. Make notes, so when the time comes you can check these details and put them to use.

Another indirect approach is to discuss a funeral you have attended together and get feedback that way. You might ask questions such as, 'Did you think all the flowers were appropriate at Aunt Mary's funeral, or should the money have been sent to her favourite charity instead?' You may feel obvious when trying to get information in this manner. That is all right. The patient is likely to be aware of what you are doing. An indirect approach allows the patient either to come out with his own choices or to go along with you in an indirect way. It is 'game-playing' that makes an unacceptable subject acceptable. Indirect approaches are not as good as an open, honest discussion – but they are much better than not dealing with it at all.

Different styles

I have seen many different approaches work. Do whatever is best for your family. Sometimes the patient may take care of the details without the carer even having to discuss it. My dad was one of these types. Being a lawyer, he was quite organized.

Many years before his death, he wrote an itemized list of every detail, numbered in the order of importance, that was to be taken care of at the time of his death. When he became ill, he updated the list and announced to the family that it would be in the top drawer of his desk. We never talked about it among ourselves, but we knew everything was in order.

When Dad died we simply went down the list and checked off the items. It was comforting to have a guide and made us feel more secure. Where Dad had no preference, he merely stated, 'as per the family's wishes'. This was a thoughtful gesture that gave us the freedom to make choices that seemed more reasonable under the circumstances.

When my aunt was diagnosed as terminal, she was quick to accept her prognosis, but her husband was not. The way we dealt with his denial was to sit down and make funeral arrangements for them both, in the event that either of them died. We put everything in writing, with detailed lists. When my aunt died everything was in good order for making decisions. We did not have to wonder about her choices.

Choices

Go over this section on choices with the patient. The major decisions are burial or cremation, viewing the body or a closed coffin, location of burial or scattering in case of cremation. It is also helpful to know the patient's preferences for church service, memorial service, private ceremony, graveside service and the denomination of the priest or pastor. Special requests as to soloist, music or ceremonies should be noted. Some people have specific desires while others do not care at all. Either way, it is best to have this information in advance.

Contacting funeral directors

I have found funeral directors and cemetery personnel exceptionally congenial. They are generally kind, thoughtful and easy to talk to.

People working in the funeral profession are accustomed to their clients being uncomfortable with the subject matter, and they make every effort to ease this discomfort. Please don't feel intimidated. If you are not treated tactfully and kindly, contact other funeral directors until you find someone who communicates easily with you. Do not hesitate to ask for items to be posted to you or for any other assistance.

If you find it too difficult to do this on your own, search for a friend who is comfortable doing this task. Hospice volunteers are well qualified to take over this job. Doctors, nurses and medical professionals who are not hospice workers are usually only focused on the healing end of illness and are not comfortable with final arrangements. Therefore, it may be wiser to look to written material, friends or hospice personnel for that information.

Services, burials, cremation, entombment

The following list touches on various choices you may be asked to make. Further explanations of terms and details follow the list.

- Traditional service followed by burial or entombment
- Traditional service followed by cremation
- Direct cremation with burial or entombment
- Direct cremation with scattering or family disposition
- Direct burial
- Memorial service
- Graveside service
- Memorial tribute

Traditional funeral

A traditional funeral is one that has a viewing, a visitation or wake, a formal service and a burial. The service and burial or entombment usually takes place the day after the viewing or visitation. If necessary, the schedule can be adjusted to allow for out-of-town relatives.

A funeral consultant advises you of your choices and provides you with a list of options and decisions that need to be made. The consultant is the person who helps you choose products and coordinate all details so the funeral runs smoothly. Choose someone who is easy to talk to and work with for both you and the patient. I have known consultants who visit the homes of terminal patients and bring catalogues with prices and pictures of all the items needed. The consultants I have worked with were tactful, considerate and applied no pressure for quick decisions.

If arrangements are made in advance, take the time to check prices and think about details. Check on your loved one's favourite poems or religious readings, type of music and choice of speakers. Determine if your loved one prefers a light-hearted celebration of life or a more formal structured service. Does he or she want a private burial?

Traditional service with cremation

Cremation is becoming more popular for ecological and financial reasons. It is a practical method and is used by many families.

A service with cremation includes a viewing and visitation period. The coffin is usually purchased. Some funeral directors offer the use of a coffin for the visitation only and then cremate in a simple container. In these cases, the cremation takes place following the service and the burial or scattering is done at a later date, either privately or with only close family members present.

Memorial service

A memorial service is usually held without the body or cremated ashes being present. It can even be held weeks after the death if necessary or desired. This is suitable if many people must travel from out of town, or in the case of a service held in a different location from where the deceased was residing. In case of cremation, most commonly a memorial service is held.

Some nice touches I have seen are displays of poster boards with collages of pictures from the person's life, and an enlarged photo of the deceased on the altar or in the reception area. At one memorial service, there was a table at the front of the church with the deceased's favourite food and memorabilia on it.

Another service I attended used the theme of the different hats worn by the deceased to tell the story of his life's accomplishments. On display in the reception area, along with photos, was a table with all his different hats, including his military cap, cowboy hat with well-worn brim and beat-up baseball cap.

Trophies or awards can be attractively arranged on the church altar or at the reception. These displays give the guests something pleasant to remember about the service and recall fond memories. Putting together these displays gives the family an opportunity to share happy memories and join in a project with a purpose. It can be fun working together on a project and it gives the family something positive to do as they search for solace.

Disposition of ashes

Ashes are typically stored in an urn. The urn is a box-type container. Various styles and prices are available from simple to elaborate. The choices usually include hand-carved oak, marble or brass. They look like vases or boxes. I recently saw what appeared to be a wooden jewellery box with the ashes stored in the bottom. You can find porcelain or ceramic figurines to express themes such as golf or a love of riding. Ashes are sealed inside. I recently saw a beautiful crystal sculpture with a frosted angel etched on it. The sculpture rested on a sterling silver stand that held the ashes.

The urn or container can be buried in the ground, just as a coffin would be, or placed in a niche (a drawer-type place inside or outside a building). A loved one can keep the urn, or the ashes can be scattered wherever it is legally allowed. Theme items or works of art can be displayed in the home.

Be aware that there are laws and restrictions on scattering ashes. Check options carefully so that no last-minute hitches occur. Scattering is not as popular as it used to be. I have heard people lament when there was no special spot for loved ones to visit following a scattering. Cemeteries are counteracting this problem by planting rose gardens for scattering. This works well because it gives the bereaved a peaceful place to visit and meditate.

Alternative burial

If you would like to arrange a burial for yourself, a friend or a family member, you can contact the Natural Death Centre for a copy of their book, *The New Natural Death Handbook*. See p. 122 for more information.

Burial

The most common place for burial is a cemetery. Sometimes burial is allowed on private property as long as permission is applied for from the local authority. People who own large tracts of land sometimes like to have their loved ones buried 'at home'. This may take some advance notice and filing of paperwork, so look into it well in advance.

I have found the staff at cemeteries to be extremely helpful and I have never had a problem getting prices and options either by telephone or by post.

The primary choices are ground burial for the coffin or urn, or a mausoleum for either of these. Other choices for ashes are a niche or scattering. Frequently, cemeteries allow loved ones to place a plaque on a tree or purchase a bench with a plaque if ashes have been scattered previously. I have seen walls with memorial plaques where no burial took place.

You may be able to obtain a single plot which can contain several urns for families who all want to be buried in one spot.

Markers come in a number of styles, from marble to bronze, small to large, single, double or family. You may desire a special message on the marker. The marker will remain for a long time, so give it careful consideration and choose something meaningful for future generations.

Cost and payment

The fact that funerals can involve large amounts of money is no secret. Most of us have heard tales of families who went so overboard on an impressive funeral that all benefits were used up to pay it off.

This is not necessary. I do not think any of us would want our loved ones going into debt over a flashy or elaborate funeral. I know one young couple, whose baby died at birth, who spent thousands on her funeral. It took them five years to pay off the loans. The young woman had to drop out of college to help make the monthly payments.

The personal touch

Many people are moving away from tradition. They are having funerals that are less a standard ritual and more a personal tribute to the individual. This personal touch brings warmth to the coldness of a funeral and adds solace.

In religions where strict rules do not need to be followed, music may be played, candles may be lit and flowers and special items may be placed around the room. The star of the local football team may be buried in his team strip with a football tucked under his arm. A soldier may be buried in full dress uniform. A cowboy can wear his plaid shirt, blue jeans and favourite hat. Children are buried with soft toys and letters from their siblings tucked beside them. One grandmother was buried in her fuzzy pink slippers and a soft, faded pink flannel nightgown. People choose whatever feels right to their family.

The most unusual funeral I heard about was held for a young man who played the drums with a band at night and was an animal trainer during the day. Surrounding his coffin at the cemetery were six fellow animal handlers with large trained felines. Off to the side was his band. They played jazz music as the large felines sat at attention. The final tune was 'When the Saints Go Marching In'. It was the perfect send-off, with red, white and blue helium balloons released as a grand finale.

Military services

Military personnel are entitled to a military funeral. It only takes a phone call to the British Legion or a local military facility to line up a bugler and chaplain, who will do the service. Grave markers are provided free of charge. A flag is draped over the coffin, then folded and presented to the next of kin as part of the service.

Photographs

Photographs are a wonderful way to celebrate a loved one's life. Display a collage of photos from happy times in the person's life, including baby pictures, wedding pictures and highlights of happy events. Sometimes just a single enlarged photo is put on display near the guest book. You may display pictures whether the coffin is open or closed. I have seen entire funeral services videotaped for those who could not be present. All these details are a matter of choice. What is acceptable and appropriate for one family may not work for another. Do whatever serves you best.

Mementoes

Funeral directors provide guest books and other items, such as orders of service or memorial bookmarks, to be given to those who attend. At the time the arrangements are made, representatives will tell you what is available. Don't be afraid to ask about cost.

The obituary

An obituary can be written by a close friend or family member and presented to the local newspaper. Some people prefer to write their own. If possible find out what your loved one feels has been most important in their life so that information can be included. Possibly a special friend could be mentioned along with relatives.

One man I knew of wanted his dog, Spike, to be included with his loved ones. Usually, what we are most proud of in our lives is not the same as what others consider our greatest accomplishments. (For example, being an author does not play as great a role in my life as being a mother and grandmother; winning a writing contest is not as important to me as having been married for more than 35 years.) Find out before the death if donations to a favourite charity are preferable to flowers. The obituary should include this information.

After the service or burial

Following the burial, most people share a meal. Friends, neighbours or church families often provide a meal at the home or at the church. Some families go to a favourite restaurant or pub, or have a catered affair. This can be a wonderful time of giving and receiving comfort. It can be a celebration of life and a time of reinforcing love.

Following a death, certain people need to be notified. They are people who have been in touch infrequently. They may not even be aware the person was ill. A short card or a photocopied note gently stating the facts can be sent after the death. Some families include the order of service from the memorial service or funeral, or a family photograph. If the patient hasn't compiled a list, check the patient's address book for names and addresses.

7

Understanding death

Death is a difficult concept for children and adults alike. I have been asked many questions about death for which there are no answers. In an attempt to discover my personal feelings, I did extensive reading and research on the subject of death.

I read numerous books on near death experiences and talked to various people who had these experiences. I was told by those who were declared dead and brought back that there are no words to describe the feelings of peace and love that surrounded them when they died. My experience with people who died from natural causes has been similar. There was a permeating feeling of serenity rather than a fearsome struggle. An indescribable feeling of peace filled the room as it became obvious that the body had been vacated.

Concepts and comparisons

While thinking about life and death, I searched for a more concrete analogy than that of a caterpillar turning into a beautiful butterfly. I began to examine seeds and plants in my garden for a new analogy. Daffodils are my favourite flowers, so I thought about the transformation a daffodil plant makes over time. The bulb is rather ugly and dried up, and appears dead. Each autumn, I carefully place daffodil bulbs in my garden and then forget about them. When spring comes, I notice tiny green shoots peeking out of the ground. Next, some leaves appear, and at last, a stem with a bulbous tip. Before very long, bright yellow daffodils cheerfully fill my garden. It's hard to believe that each pretty little flower started out from a dried bulb that rested quietly in the ground all through the winter!

The daffodil is the first flower of spring, the flower of hope. And it *does* bring hope after the long, cold and often dreary winter months.

It is not possible for us to explain or fully understand the transformation of a seed or bulb. I only know I see it repeated year after year and know it is possible. We simply must have faith that the seed or bulb will fulfil its promises after it is planted, and change from one state to another.

Likewise, I have watched people in the last days of their lives change

111

greatly. They may have lost their attractive looks, control of their bodily functions and their productive careers. Yet they were still filled with love, tranquillity and grace. It emanated from their eyes and was in their touch. They had reached the point where they realized this life on earth was coming to an end and they moved forward gently, with great dignity. What a gift to be able to spend whatever time is remaining with them in an atmosphere of love and serenity!

Planning for the death

Thinking about the time of death and planning for it in advance is not morbid. It is a necessary task – a time of preparation that makes the actual moment less stressful and emotional. Preparation prevents confusion and chaos and brings loved ones together to support each other and ease the pain.

Many months are spent planning for the birth of a baby. Mother and father plan and prepare for the infant's arrival so that it goes smoothly. Death is the other end of life's spectrum. It is just as natural as birth and an inevitable moment for each of us. By thinking about it and making necessary decisions in advance, it can be a time of reinforcing love and of allowing a natural transition.

Physical signs of approaching death

The body's systems begin to shut down as the patient becomes sicker. Certain signs are present during the last few days of life. Fear of the unknown is always great, so I want to be as open and honest with you as possible about these signs. The following information will help you prepare for, anticipate and understand symptoms you may observe as your loved one approaches the final stage of life.

Even though you have been caring for the patient and discussing the possibility of death, it can still be a shock when the time actually comes. By being tuned in to the physical changes involved, you can be better equipped emotionally.

Not all of these symptoms are present in every patient, and some may not be experienced at all. Some patients slip into a comatose or semi-comatose state for one to three days prior to death and others may take a final breath in the middle of a sentence.

The following list is adapted from one used by the Antelope Valley Visiting Nurses Hospice Organization and ProCare Hospice.

Symptoms of approaching death and what to do to add comfort

The following list describes symptoms to watch for in the patient and comfort measures to provide in each case.

- The patient may begin to sleep more and become difficult to awaken. Usually this is the result of metabolic changes. Plan activities and communication at times when the patient seems more alert.
- Your loved one may be confused about the time, where they are and the identity of people. This is also the result of metabolic changes. Gently correct the patient but do not be unduly concerned about the confusion.
- Loss of control of bowel and bladder may occur as the nervous system changes. Place pads under the patient. Ask your medical professional about information on skin hygiene and the appropriateness of a catheter.
- Arms and legs may become cool to the touch; the underside of the body may become darker as circulation slows. Keep the patient warm with extra blankets. Do not use electric blankets, which can injure tissue that has become fragile.
- Secretions may collect in the back of the throat, causing noisy breathing. This is called the death rattle and it may last for days. Use a cool humidifier in the room. Elevate the head of the bed or add extra pillows. Moisten the mouth with ice cubes or a moist washcloth if the patient is able to swallow. Reposition the patient onto their side.
- Hearing and vision will lessen as the nervous system slows down. Keep the lights on in the room. Never assume a patient cannot hear. Talk as if hearing is intact and be very cautious about side conversations in the room.
- The patient may be restless, pull at bed linens, have visions or call out. This is the result of less oxygen getting to the brain. Stay calm, speak slowly and assuredly. Do not leave the patient alone if they are showing signs of distress.
- Your loved one will not want food or fluids as the need for these decreases. Moisten mouth with a moist cloth. Clean the mouth every 30 minutes to two hours with wet cotton swabs. Keep lips moist with a lip balm.
- As a result of dehydration, a sweet odour may be present. Keep the premises as clean and well-aired as possible without chilling the patient.
- You may notice irregular breathing patterns, and there may be spaces of time for ten to 30 seconds with no breathing. Elevate the head by raising the bed or using pillows.

- Hearing is the last sense to leave a person. Even when people are comatose, they can still hear, so continue to speak lovingly and gently when in their presence, offering confirmations that you will be all right when they leave you.

Timing

Hospice workers have discovered that people have a certain degree of control over choosing the time of their actual death. I would not have believed this phenomenon if I had not seen it for myself many times. I watched a man delay his death, which by all medical terms should not have been possible, until his tax forms were completed.

I watched a woman live for months while she waited for her husband to learn how to cook and run the household adequately. Hospice workers have all seen patients linger until a specific family member appeared at the bedside to say farewell, until after a holiday or other special event, and even until after the birth of a grandchild.

Giving 'permission' to die

Often people wait to die until they receive permission from their loved ones. Patients often cannot relax enough to take their final breaths until they know their families are going to manage without them.

If your loved one is lingering longer than their medical team feels is comfortable, consider telling him or her that they do not have to worry about you; assure them that they may leave. Try not to act in a manner that makes the patient think he or she has to remain for your sake. At this point, pain control may be the best it is going to be and it may be time to say goodbye. Add reassurances of love and special messages of encouragement so that they can drift off peacefully.

Children

Statistics show that children rarely die when their parents are in the room. It is as if they realize it would simply be too painful for their parents to witness. Children wait for days until the parents sneak out for a bite to eat or to take a shower, and then they take their last breaths. If you happen not to be present at the actual time of death, do not feel guilty or be alarmed. This is the way it was meant to be.

After the death

When a death takes place at home, the carer is in charge. It is not necessary to rush around and do anything. Instead, try to stay calm and console anyone else present. Many families wish to bathe their loved one, change the deceased's clothing and bedding, and gather together special people to say farewell in the privacy of a familiar environment.

I have been in households where the minister and family members were called and they all spent time in prayer before telephoning the undertakers to take their loved one away to be prepared for a formal funeral.

I have seen a wife trim her deceased husband's beard before notifying the undertaker. Another time, two daughters insisted on photographs with their father before he was taken to be cremated. People may wish to cut off a lock of hair or sprinkle a favourite perfume on the body. All these acts are fine.

Each death is unique

Do not worry about anyone judging what you do. Each death is a unique experience. Be true to your natural reactions. Spending quiet time and saying a final goodbye can ease the pain of separation and begin the grief process in a normal, natural manner. There is no rush to have your loved one removed from your home. This may be your last private time together, so use it productively. It might take three or four hours to gather loved ones who wish to say private goodbyes, and that's all right too.

Whom to call

If you are not working with hospice, look into the necessary procedure to follow. Ask your doctor about the best procedure and check with the coroner's office ahead of time.

Closure

Years ago, families always handled funerals at home without professional help. Male members built the wooden coffin and women prepared the body. Children were on the scene, helping when necessary. The wake took place in the parlour, and the burial was often in the far pasture. Today, we have professionals handle the details and we deny ourselves the feeling of natural closure.

Many times, families are left at loose ends after the death of their loved one, especially the people who have been involved in caring. They feel left out and wonder, 'Is this all there is?' Take your time turning your loved one over to professionals to ensure you are prepared to let go.

Often, having a signed statement from a doctor declaring the patient is terminally ill suffices and resuscitation measures can be omitted. The death certificate needs to be signed by the doctor. The hospice volunteer may help prepare the body and call the undertaker. The volunteer can be a soothing, experienced influence who can take charge. If hospice is not on the scene, someone else needs to take over this job and organize matters.

Death in the hospital

If your loved one is in hospital or a convalescent home when death occurs, you can still ask for some quiet, private time alone before the staff remove the body. You may have to be firm and insistent, but remember, this is the only chance you may have to say goodbye privately.

Bereavement

Grief is the emotional response to a loss. Bereavement is the period of time following a major loss, and mourning is the process that brings about acceptance. If you have been the main carer during a terminal illness, you may feel lost at first. Be aware that you will not always feel this way. Take your time as you tenderly ease yourself back into activities you enjoyed before becoming a carer.

Looking back on the days when I was caring for my parents, I find little sprinkles of joy. I remember the midnight snacks of milk and cookies with my mother, and telling her she was the best mother anyone could have ever had. She seemed to surprised and responded by telling me *I* was the best daughter a mother could ever want.

My dad, who seemed so preoccupied with his career when I was a young child, bathed me in love during the final month of his life. All the praise I had needed as a child was lavished on me. It made up for all the insecurities I suffered as I was growing up. I knew how much I had been loved all those years, whether it was verbally expressed or not. Every day Dad made sure he told me how much he loved me, over and over again.

Being a carer is certainly draining, but, oh, the joyful returns!

Feeling relief

If you feel relieved following the death of your loved one, do not feel guilty. This is a normal reaction after a long illness. It is also natural to feel relief that your loved one is no longer ill. And it is natural to be relieved that you can now resume your normal life. On top of this, you may be exhausted after months of giving care. Relief that the situation has changed is perfectly normal.

If you have concerns about your feelings, discuss them with the hospice team. They are familiar with these reactions and will be glad to listen as you work them out. If you were not involved with hospice, find an understanding friend who will listen as you express your feelings. Or join a grief support group. Internet chat rooms are becoming a popular way to receive support. Research all available resources.

Talk and write about grief

Grief takes great amounts of energy and cannot be hurried through. When it arrives after the care of a terminal patient, there is usually no energy left in reserve. The adjustment takes time, so do not expect to jump back to normal activity overnight. The best therapy for grief is talking about your feelings. The second-best one is writing about them. Do one or the other, or both, until you feel good again. Don't rush your feelings.

Try to live one day at a time. Do not make elaborate plans too far in advance. Read some helpful books on grief. Look up good friends and spend time doing fun activities with them. Laugh, swim and eat luxurious meals. Buy a new outfit, go to the mountains and build a snowman. Just enjoy every hour of each day, remembering to treat yourself tenderly. Take it easy and do a lot of pampering. Lower your expectations, and spend quiet time in prayer and meditation, letting your faith guide you.

People who have had the privilege of caring for their loved one during a final illness find rewards that far outweigh the suffering. Be reassured you will have happy memories to review and a great feeling of accomplishment. You have given an irreplaceable gift of love to someone and can feel good about it for the rest of your life. Hold on to that thought and let it console you in the days ahead.

Further reading

General

Bettelheim, Bruno, *The Informed Heart*. Pelican, Gretna, LA, 1988.

du Boulay, Shirley, *Cicely Saunders: The Founder of the Modern Hospice Movement*. Hodder & Stoughton, London, 1987.

Brooker, Tim, *Signs of Life*. Times, Maryland, 1997.

Chesser, E., *Living With Suicide*. Hutchinson, London, 1967.

Eareckson Tada, Joni, *When Is It Right to Die?* Zondervan, Grand Rapids, Michigan, 1992.

Golden, Thomas R., *Swallowed by a Snake: The Gift of the Masculine Side of Healing*. Golden Healing Publishing, Maryland, 1996. Addresses the different ways in which men and women grieve.

Holman, Patricia, *Holding On: The True Story of a Mother's Loss of Her Only Child and Her Husband*. Unicorn Press, London, 1997.

Kübler-Ross, Elisabeth, *Aids: The Ultimate Challenge*. Pocket Books, UK, 1997.

Kübler-Ross, Elisabeth, *Death: The Final Stage of Growth*. Pocket Books, UK, 1997.

Kübler-Ross, Elisabeth, *Living with Death and Dying*. Pocket Books, UK, 1997.

Kushner, Harold, *When Bad Things Happen to Good People*. Pan, London, 1982.

Perry, Gail and Jill Perry (eds), *A Rumour of Angels: Quotations for Living, Dying and Letting Go*. Ballantine, New York, 1989.

Raphael, B., *When Disaster Strikes*. Hutchinson, London, 1986.

Savan, Anne, *Battered Brass*. Taliesin Publishing, UK, 1997. Poems of bereavement by a bereaved parent. Possibly not for the newly bereaved.

Stearns, Anne Kaiser, *Living Through a Personal Crisis*. Ballantine, New York, 1988.

For carers

Ainsworth-Smith, Ian and Peter Speck, *Letting Go: Caring for the Dying and Bereaved*. SPCK, London, second edition, 1999.

Byock, Ira, *Dying Well*. Riverhead Books, New York, 1997. The inside story of hospice and its success.

Callanan, Maggie and Patricia Kelley, *Final Gifts*. Poseidon Press, New York, 1992. Understanding special needs and communication with the dying.

Duda, Deborah, *Coming Home: A Guide to Dying at Home with Dignity*. Aurora Press, New York, 1987. Practical suggestions to make the final weeks as comfortable as possible.

Grollman, Earl, *Caring and Coping When Your Loved One is Seriously Ill*. Beacon Press, Boston, MA, 1995. Sensible, practical and compassionate wisdom from a rabbi.

Kolf, June Cerza, *How Can I Help? How to Support Someone Who is Grieving*. Fisher Books, Tucsan, Arizona, 1999.

Neuberger, Julia, *Caring for Dying People of Different Faiths*. Austen Cornish, in association with the Lisa Sainsbury Foundation, 1987.

Stoddard, Sandol, *The Hospice Movement – A Better Way of Caring for the Dying*. Random House, New York, 1978. The history and philosophy of the hospice movement.

For children

Grollman, Earl, *Explaining Death to Children*. Beacon Press, Boston, MA, 1965. An easy to read, well-written book to help understand how grief affects children.

Mellonie, Bryan and Robert Ingpen, *Lifetimes: A Beautiful Way to Explain Death to Children*. Bantam, New York, 1983. A colourful storybook to read to young children.

Oyler, Chris, *Go Toward the Light*. Harper & Row, New York, 1988. Insightful information by the mother of a seven year old with AIDS, his diagnosis, illness and death.

Schaefer, Dan and Christine Lyons, *How Do We Tell the Children? A Parent's Guide to Helping Children Understand and Cope When*

Someone Dies. Newmarket Press, New York, 1986. Everything a person needs to know about dealing with children of all ages and death. Special crisis section for quick reference.

On-line resources

Amazon Books
http://www.amazon.co.uk
Books in every category. Easy to order; well-organized lists.

Growth House
http://www.growthhouse.org
Extensive site with resources and chat rooms on death and grief.

Useful addresses

The Befriending Network
11 St Bernard's Road
Oxford OX2 6EH
Tel: 01865 316200
A nationwide network providing trained volunteers who visit the homes of the critically ill to relieve carers by running errands and sitting with the person who is ill.

Carers National Association
20–25 Glasshouse Yard
London EC1A 4JS
Tel: 020 7490 8818
Fax: 020 7490 8824
Helpline: 0345 573 369
Aims to help anyone whose life is restricted because of the need to take responsibility for a person whose health is impaired by sickness or age.

The Compassionate Friends
53 North Street
Bristol BS3 1EN
Tel: 0117 9539 639 (helpline)
Fax: 0117 9665 202
TCF offers friendship and understanding to other bereaved parents, with links around the world. TCF has a postal library with more than 900 book titles, including a wide range of books for children.

CRUSE Bereavement Care
CRUSE House
126 Sheen Road
Richmond TW9 1UR
Tel: 020 8940 4818
Extensive lists of publications on bereavement available for carers and for all affected by bereavement.

London Bereavement Network
356 Holloway Road
London N7 6PN
Tel: 020 7700 8134
Fax: 020 7700 8146
email: lbn@bereavement.demon.co.uk

National Federation of Spiritual Healers
Old Manor Farm Studio
Church Street
Sunbury on Thames TW16 6RG
Tel: 01932 783 164

The Natural Death Centre
20 Heber Road
London NW2 6AA
Tel: 020 8208 2853
Fax: 020 8452 6434
email: rhino@dial.pipex.com
website: http://www.worldtrans.org/naturaldeath.html
A non-profit charitable project launched in 1991. Aims to support those
dying at home and their carers to help them arrange funerals. A more
general aim of helping improve the 'quality of dying'.

Princess Royal Trust for Carers
16 Byward Street
Tower Hill
London EC3R 5BA
Tel: 020 7480 7788
Fax: 020 7481 4729
Supports a national network of Carers Centres where carers of all kinds
can obtain advice, information and support.

The Samaritans (A member of Befrienders International)
10 The Grove
Slough SL1 1QP
Tel: 01753 216500
Fax: 01753 819004
Linkline: 0345 909090
website: http://www.samaritans.org.uk

AIDS

National AIDS Helpline: 0800 567 123

Terrence Higgins Trust
52–54 Grays Inn Road
London WC1X 8JU
Tel: 020 7831 0330
Helpline: 020 7242 1010
email: info@tht.org.uk

Cancer

Bacup
3 Bath Place
Rivington Street
London EC2A 3JR
Tel: Cancer Information Service Freeline 0800 800 1234
Helps people with cancer, their families and friends, live with cancer.

Hospice Information Service
51 Lawrie Park Road
London SE26 6DZ
Tel: 020 8778 9252
Fax: 020 8776 9345
email: his@stchris.ftech.co.uk
The Hospice Information Service exists to benefit both public and health professionals. A directory of hospice services in the UK and Ireland can be obtained by sending a large sae to the above address.

Imperial Cancer Research Fund
PO Box 123
Lincoln's Inn Fields
London WC2A 3PX
Tel: 020 7242 0200

Macmillan Cancer Relief
Anchor House
15–19 Britten Street
London SW3 3TZ
Tel: 020 7351 7811
Supports and develops services to provide specialist care for people with cancer at every stage of their illness.

World Cancer Research Fund
105 Park Street
London W1Y 3FB
Tel: 020 7343 4200

Children

The Association of Children's Hospices
c/o Hope House
Nant Lane, Morda
nr Oswestry
Shropshire SY10 9BX
Tel: 01691 671999
Fax: 01691 679465
email: xhopehouse@aol.com

Jessie's Fund
10 Bootham Terrace
York YO30 7DH
Tel/Fax: 01904 658189
email: jessiefund@aol.com
Jessie's Fund is dedicated to helping, through music, children who have special needs as a result of illness or disability. Jessie's Fund is primarily, though not exclusively, involved in encouraging and promoting music therapy in children's hospices.

Index